Private Splendor

Great Families at Home

Alexis Gregory

Marc Walter

The Vendome Press

Contents

6   KASTEEL DE HAAR

28   CASA DE PILATOS

52   HAREWOOD HOUSE

82   CHÂTEAU DE HAROUÉ

106   PALAZZO GANGI

132   PALAZZO SACCHETTI

156   SCHLOSS ST. EMMERAM

184   PALÁCIO FRONTEIRA

206   Acknowledgments

Kasteel de Haar

A Dutch Baron's Dream Castle near Utrecht

Kasteel de Haar, the largest castle in Holland, is the product of a marriage between two dynasties, one aristocratic the other financial. Baron Etienne van Zuylen van Nyevelt van de Haar (page 13) was the scion of a grand and ancient Dutch family whose castle had been ravaged several times during Holland's turbulent history. Tall, elegant, and extremely determined, he nurtured a dream to rebuild his family's ruined castle on an even grander scale, wanting to create "a museum like Pierrefonds, but still comfortable to live in during the month of August." He married one of Europe's greatest heiresses, Hélène de Rothschild, known as "la belle Hélène (page 16)," the only child of Baron Salomon de Rothschild, whose mother and father were cousins. Family policy imposed what might be considered today slightly incestuous alliances in order to keep the Rothschild fortune under their control, so Hélène had a double infusion of Rothschild riches. Soon after they married, Hélène asked Etienne what he most wanted in the whole world; he told her of his dream, and she made it come true. Built in the lowlands surrounding Utrecht, very little of the original castle remained. Before the baron started rebuilding it in 1892, travelers looking for old and romantic sights could visit the very impressive ruins of the van Zuylen feudal castle, one of the most important in the region. Some walls of the main building as well as imposing towers had resisted the ravages of time, and still dominated the surrounding countryside. The large courtyard was hidden under rubble, and among the weeds and brambles stood a solitary elm, which spread its large branches and leaves over what remained of the heavy masonry. The cellars had caved in but a few of the old vaults remained; some of the large, now ceiling-less rooms preserved remnants of their fireplaces; and traces of beams could be seen as well as vestiges of architectural ornamentation on the second floor. The thick towers and walls made it possible to see where the castles defenses had been, and although the castle had suffered mightily from wars, fires, the ravages of weather, abandonment, and looting by disrespectful and ignorant visitors, it still made a very powerful impression.

It is generally agreed that the Kasteel de Haar, referred to by the present owner and his friends as simply "the Haar," was built, or at least lived in, as of 1162 by Godschalk, the brother of Herman, Lord of Woerden, whose family took on Haar as a family name and owned the castle until 1446. Haar is derived from a Saxon word describing a significant piece of uncultivated land higher than the terrain surrounding it. It is these characteristics that encouraged the building of a fortress for protecting the only access between the Rhine and Vecht rivers from Normans, pirates, and other invaders. The two rivers

(Preceding pages) The immense, Gothic Revival Kasteel de Haar near Utrecht in Holland seems to be arriving, through the early autumn mist, like a giant contemporaneous luxury liner. To the left can be seen the castle's chapel. Referred to by family and friends as "The Haar," the castle shares with those behemoths of the sea, an unparalleled life of luxury, detachment from reality, separation from land, and nostalgia for the past. Visitors cross the moat on a drawbridge that can still be pulled up (above), and they immediately encounter a coat of arms with the van Zuylen motto "Non titubans" or "never wavering." They enter through the main, wrought-iron door (opposite) designed like everything else in the house by P. J. H. Cuypers, the architect. One of the carriages of the castle's first owner (above).

linked Utrecht and Haarlem, both important commercial centers. In 1176 and 1177, Elias de Haar was the Great Bailiff of Utrecht, one of the most important people in Holland, and his role validated the castle as a lordly residence. The last Lord of the Haar had two children: Werner, who died shortly after maturity, and Jospina, who inherited everything from her brother and married Baron Thierry van Zuylen in 1434. It was then that the two titles were linked and the castle became known as Haarzuilens, as did an adjacent village that was put up to house the tenant farmers that Etienne van Zuylen had to displace when he rebuilt the castle and created a large park at the end of the nineteenth century. During Baron Thierry's lifetime, there was great instability in Holland between many who felt that the political system had to be completely overhauled in order to adapt to great economic changes, and others who were for the status quo. The Cabillauds were the party of change and the Hoecks were the traditionalists. The Cabillauds advocated foreign intervention and supported the invasion of the Duke of Burgundy who made his son David Prince Bishop of Utrecht in 1456. The bishop asked the Dutch government to oust the Hoeck party and seize the Haar, since Baron van Zuylen, then mayor of Utrecht, was the leading opponent of the Burgundians. There was a great battle, and

When Baron Etienne van Zuylen, seen right, with his architect decided to transform the ruins of his family's castle into Holland's largest and most luxurious castle, thanks to the financial support of the Rothschild heiress he married, he moved local farmers who had put up small houses to a nearby village built by Cuypers, and transformed the fields into an enormous park. He brought in literally hundreds of mature chestnut trees and oaks, excavated a long water allée (above) that he lined with statuary and, upon the premature death of his son, Hélin, created a wonderful rose garden in his memory. Soon came a tennis court, deer park, and stables for his carriage horses.

the castle was destroyed. It was rebuilt a half century later, only to be partially destroyed again during the invasion of King Louis XIV, whose soldiers used it as a prison until the Treaty of Nymenghen brought peace in 1677.

Thereafter, the van Zuylens no longer lived on their land, and rented out small plots near the castle to local farmers who built modest houses, and their black and white cows happily grazed in the fields. Baron Etienne, the grandfather of the present owner, became an absentee landlord, living between Brussels and Paris. In the course of his leisurely life, he founded the French Automobile Club in the days when the motorcar was considered a touring and racing vehicle for the super rich. A kind man, he loved horses and wanted to encourage the automobile since he felt it was an invention that would make their lives easier. Although the Baron's ties to Holland had become somewhat tenuous, his vision of a dream castle became obsessive. He fancied a place where he would invite his friends from *le tout Paris*, the group of super-refined and beautifully dressed aristocrats, literati, and captains of industry who relished nothing more than *le bon mot*, costume balls, gossip, and scandal—the French society so well described by Marcel Proust. In Paris, they gathered at the Jockey Club and on the racecourse, paraded in their polished carriages on the Avenue du Bois (a favorite occupation of Baron Etienne), entertained their mistresses at Maxim's, and followed the social seasons from London to Cairo. In the summer, they took the waters to recover from the excesses of the winter and, in the fall, they château-hopped to shooting parties. Etienne must have felt inadequate at his inability to reciprocate in the style in which he was received, particularly in view of his long lineage. He therefore chose the path of several of his elegant European contemporaries, and began searching for a great heiress who would pay for his castle.

The second half of the nineteenth century was a time of social upheaval. The income from ancient estates plummeted in the face of new wealth. Aristocratic families may have held onto their properties, but they were short of cash. Newly rich industrialists were rapidly entering their privileged world, the richest coming from the New World. Robber barons from New York and Cleveland and Pittsburgh who had made vast fortunes in railroads, steel mills, mines, and mass production proliferated like mushrooms thanks to the Industrial Revolution. Along with these industrialists came the bankers and financiers such as J. P. Morgan and Jacob Schiff. But they were small fry indeed compared to the Rothschilds, the greatest financial dynasty since the Medicis. And the Dutch

baron was very fortunate to have met and fallen in love with Baroness Hélène de Rothschild. Her family coat of arms included five arrows, representing the five sons of the patriarch, Meyer Amschel Rothschild—a Yiddish-speaking Frankfurt moneychanger who made his fortune out of a friendship with the Duke of Hess Cassel. Meyer Amschel sent his sons to establish banks in Frankfurt, London, Paris, Naples, and Vienna, creating the first multinational business. All the sons were bright, but the true financial geniuses were Nathan in London and Jacob (who Anglicized his name to James) in Paris. James had two sons and a daughter. From a Rothschild family perspective, Hélène's marriage to a Christian Dutch baron was not ideal, but Etienne prevailed over any family criticism; her father was dead, the couple was in love, and they soon produced two sons, first Hélin and then Egmont.

Now married to one of the world's great heiresses, Etienne persuaded Hélène to share his dream, and he set out to rebuild the family castle he so longed for. Settling for nothing but the best, he approached P. J. H. Cuypers, the most renowned architect in the Netherlands, who restored Munster Cathedral in Roermond and St. Servaas in Maastricht, and had built from scratch Amsterdam's Rijksmuseum and Central Station. Like France's Eugène-Emmanuel Viollet-le-Duc, the restorer of the Château de Pierrefonds and the cathedral of Nôtre Dame in Paris, Cuypers was a leading protagonist of the Gothic Revival. With the foundations of the castle's destroyed walls to build on, he obviously used the Dutch Gothic architectural vocabulary that was at his fingertips. There were many contemporary Gothic manors and castles in the neighborhood, and he was free to hire the finest sculptors, wood carvers, stained-glass makers, and interior decorators of the time. Cuypers himself designed every detail in the house, from the wooden wainscoting to the silverware, and the château was so large that he set up a brick factory on the property using the local earth, so that every brick would be of the same hue. Meanwhile, the baron and baroness traveled around the Orient buying dozens of magnificent Japanese Imari vases and lacquer pieces. Upon their return, they frequented the renowned Duveen galleries, where they bought a famous set of Gobelin tapestries, Old Master paintings, Dutch furniture, and Oriental carpets to decorate their castle.

The turn of the century was a period when great revivalist palaces were being built in Newport, New York, and in Europe. Of course, the Rothschilds were the great palace builders of the period, as attested by Mentmore, Waddesdon Manor, and the Château de Ferrières. Consequently, the Kasteel de Haar is very much part of this contemporary castle-building mania. If the Rothschilds were not thrilled that Hélène had married out of the faith, they must have been secretly pleased and proud that she was so closely linked to the sort of master building they adored.

Baron Etienne began his project by moving all his tenants to Haarzuilens, the small village Cuypers built nearby. He paid

A Gothic statue (opposite), bathed in the setting sun, stands in the small entrance of the castle, as does a bust of Baron Étienne van Zuylen (right). The baron's family is memorialized in the family chapel (above), where everybody gathers for mass on Sunday. There are inscribed plaques in the nave with the names and coats of arms of all the van Zuylens, the sepulchres of Etienne and his wife Hélène (née de Rothschild) are in the nave, while those of his son Egmont and his wife Marguerite are in the crypt below. (Overleaf), The spectacular main entrance hall, which was the original courtyard of the castle, soars the entire height of the massive building, and is covered with neo-Gothic figures and reliefs. Etienne placed here many of his most important paintings, statues, furniture, and large Chinese vases.

The bust of baroness Hélène (left), whose fortune made the castle a reality, is in the billiard room (above and opposite). The Ballroom, or Salle de Fêtes (overleaf), is one of the most beautiful—and least used—rooms of the château. At one far end of the hall, unseen here, is a delicate marble filigree covered gallery for musicians to play, and above the windows, with their linen fold shutters and lining, are white marble singing and dancing angels highlighted in gold leaf. Baron Etienne's portrait is at the other end of the room. The oak ceiling is sculpted with various flora and fauna and hides electric lights, which illuminate the important Renaissance tapestries that hang on walls upholstered in harmonious red velvet.

for the new houses as he knocked the old ones down to clear his land and plant a large, formal French garden in the style of André Le Nôtre, the great gardener of Louis XIV. A long water allée (page 11) now stretches on one side of the castle where a family of swans, led by the particularly ferocious "Hitler" who guides his spouse and cygnets along the algae-coated water. On another side is an exquisite rose garden that Hélène had planted to commemorate the untimely death of their adored oldest son Hélin in an automobile accident in 1912. Their grief is poignantly recorded in a dedication carved on a marble column that speaks of the flowers representing so many rose-cheeked young men who died premature deaths, rather eerily foreseeing the catastophic loss of life in the world war that would start two years later. On the third side, overlooking the road where passersby have a splendid view of the looming castle, is a lovely series of trimmed boxwood bushes and carefully kept flower parterres.

The castle's drawbridge over the moat to the main entrance (page 8) overlooks a circular flowered parterre, beyond which lie a deer park and a forest of oaks and chestnut trees planted by the baron, many already mature. The moat is extended on the rose garden side into a small lake that reflects, mirror-like, this astonishing Romantic castle in its still, dark waters. In

addition to the castle, often referred to by the Francophile van Zuylens as "le château," Cuypers designed a smaller châtelet whose rooms shelter the family when they have closed the château for the season. The château, with its many bedrooms, large and soaring Gothic hall, escutcheon-covered living room, library, ballroom, billiard room, formal dining room (seating up to forty guests), and writing and card room, were used for house parties during the summer months and early autumn. Etienne and Hélène's many guests would motor up from Paris, a voyage of a few days at the time, and stay several weeks. Now, the house parties take place only during September, when the house is closed to visitors (it is one of the most visited tourist sites in Holland), and consist of long weekends for the guests and the entire month for the baron. The family banner, consisting of the red towers of the family crest on a white field, along with their motto "non titubans" or "never wavering," flies from a turret when the present baron is in residence, as it did for his parents and grandparents when these legendary house parties were taking place. An invitation to a Haar house party has always been coveted and cherished.

After Hélin's premature death, the château passed to Baron Etienne's second son, Egmont, an astonishing figure in many ways. He was so distinguished in appearance, comportment, and dress that all heads turned as he entered a room or took a stroll. Well over two meters in height, he stood ramrod straight, wore his abundant hair *en brosse*, sported a luxuriant though small moustache, and generally had a monocle secured firmly over his left eye. He was made for a court uniform and medals, which he wore in the diplomatic service of Belgium's king, and he remained active in foreign affairs throughout his life. He later served on the Belgian delegation to the United Nations, founded and edited several literary and political magazines, was an avid golfer, and a leading figure in Europe's racing world under the family's red and white colors.

He had been engaged, at his father's insistence, to Princess Marina of Greece before leaving for a post at the Belgian embassy in Cairo. There he fell in love with the Egyptian beauty Marguerite Namétallah who, along with her sister Maria, were adored in Egypt's highly refined, land-owning, and cotton-growing society of pashas, beys, and effendis. Marguerite, known to her friends as Maggie, loved nothing more than telling exaggerated tales of her impoverished childhood, tales that were belied by the fact that she belonged to a sufficiently elevated strata of Cairo's snobbish society to meet the renowned and much-heralded Egmont van Zuylen. Maggie had jet-black hair, lovely, green, laughing eyes, and a natural intelligence that her good friend André Malraux described as the most acute he had ever encountered. She spoke French with the lilting cadence and inflection of the Levant, and told her highly amusing stories in a sort of throaty gasp. She was pure Lawrence Durrell, an exotic creature akin to a sleek, black panther, and Egmont's father was not at all pleased with his son

Guests gather in the Knights Hall (opposite), the main living room of the château, for a whisky sour or glass of champagne before dinner. They also gather here for afternoon tea, a game of chess (right), a bit of bridge at the card table, or a conversation on one of the Gothic chairs. On the ceiling, the beams are decorated with painted coats of arms of the various van Zuylen family lines and inlaid wood Stars of David representing Baroness Hélène de Rothschild. When Maria Callas stayed here, she would occasionally sing to her own accompaniment, using the grand piano. Off the Knights Hall is a room where high-stake poker is regularly played (overleaf, left), and a smaller Family Room with another carved fireplace is filled to capacity with family genealogy (overleaf, right).

Off the soaring main entrance hall is the dining room (above), one of Cuypers' delightful Gothic Revival fantasies, where twenty-four guests sit down every night when the baron has a house party. At the far end is a black marble fireplace, the symbol of family life, whose lintel is inscribed in gold lettering. It is surmounted by carved white marble scenes of Adam and Eve in Paradise and of the marriages of Isaac and Rebecca and of Tobias and Sarah. Cuypers personally designed everything here: the linen-fold panels, bronze chandelier, candlesticks, and silverware with the family arms *(opposite)*. Footmen pass around heavy silver platters laid out by the French chefs. The guest book (left).

for changing the dynastic plan he had so carefully marked out. Egmont and Maggie had three children: Marie-Hélène, the eldest, who was to become the queen of Paris society due to the legendary balls she gave as the wife of Baron Guy de Rothschild; a second daughter Sybil who died in childhood; and a son, the present Baron Thierry, known to his many friends as Teddy. Teddy inherited his parents' striking features and character in equal measure, certainly his mother's wit and his father's distinction. Harvard-educated, he spent most of his childhood in New York and Santa Barbara, and he developed his father's passion for politics (though of a much more liberal bent), literature, race horses, and, above all, for the château. One of Teddy's greatest accomplishments has been opening the château to the public while conserving its private character. Teddy presides over a new foundation, directed by Holland's most distinguished business figures, which provides him and his heirs use, in perpetuity, of the château in September and the châtelet throughout the year.

In the first days of September, a large and devoted staff of maids, butlers, chefs, and chauffeurs is assembled, and beautiful bouquets are placed around the reception rooms and bedrooms, which range in style from the Ritz in Paris to Claridge's in London, from Charles V to Olde Holland. The sheets are

Several bedrooms in the Dutch style are located in the garret off a narrow corridor. Guests up here are occasionally disturbed by bats flying around outside their rooms as they make their way to their bathrooms in the corridor (above). As a consequence, these rooms are reserved for habitués of the castle! There are a host of bedrooms in the château and the adjacent châtelet, which is reached through a covered bridge. The most luxurious bedrooms are the ones Baron Etienne created for himself, a Gothic Revival suite with carved marble fireplace, statuary, and a sumptuous carved wood Gothic bed, and the pale pink and white chamber he created for his wife. It looks as if it could have been taken straight out of the Paris Ritz, built at about the same time. (Opposite) One of the bathrooms in the Tower wing where the tubs are filled every evening for the guests. Bicycles are set out every day so that guests can ride around the extensive grounds (left).

aired, beds made, and pillows plumped. The French chefs start on their sauces and sugar sculptures, and the staff puts out a dozen bicycles for the guests. A grand piano arrives, on which one of the baron's musical protégés will give a concert in the Gothic hall, and the cars gear up to fetch guests at the airport from all over Europe and the United States. Gasps are the inevitable reaction of first-time visitors, who are immediately put at ease by the baron as he leads them to the living room, where the beams bear the family crests and Hélène's Star of David. Shortly, the guests proceed to their rooms to change into their black ties, evening gowns, and best jewels after a hot bath in an enormous British tub exported to Holland at the beginning of the nineteenth century. Cuypers even put heating under the bathrooms' marble floors (above), an unheard of luxury at the time. A gong shortly resounds throughout the castle from the great hall (pages 14, 15), summoning everybody to the living room for whisky sours and champagne before dinner. Thus begins a weekend filled with good conversation, delicious food and drink, golf and tennis, excursions to look at Rembrandts and other paintings at the Mauritshuis in the Hague or the Rijksmuseum in Amsterdam, rides around the property on bicycles, long walks, concerts, and poker games.

The château is remarkable in many ways, but most extraordinary is its continuity. From the moment a guest has the good fortune to cross the drawbridge, he is back in the days of Etienne and Hélène, with standards of hospitality and a life style that disappeared after World War I. Time takes on a new dimension, current events seem faraway on another planet, work and worry become an activity of other, lesser mortals, and the seating plan for dinner takes on immense importance. On Sunday morning before lunch, there has always been mass in the family chapel (page 13). Its walls are decorated with marble bas reliefs, inscribing the genealogy of the van Zuylen family. In the apse are the stately tombs of Etienne, Hélin, and Hélène, and in the crypt are those of Egmont, Maggie, and other family members. When the mass ends and the doors are locked until the next Sunday, it is more than possible that there is a discussion among all the van Zuylens as to whether Teddy's weekend and guests are up to the high standards set in the past. The answer is invariably positive.

CASA DE PILATOS

Miraculous Marriage of Antiquity, Islam, and the West

The historic center of Seville, rich in convents and churches, is replete with magnificent private palaces that still belong to members of Spain's leading aristocratic families who once owned most of the land on the Iberian peninsula and played a leading role in the nation's history. One member of this illustrious class is the present Duchess of Medinaceli(page 47), whose ancestors built up the great house known as the Casa de Pilatos or House of Pilate. It is one of the most visited monuments in Seville. One ancestor of the Duchess, it is rumored, was a backer of Christopher Columbus's expeditions, which would explain why there are ears of corn in the family coat of arms. If that is indeed the case, he would have been in charge of the discovery of America!

Thanks to the gold and silver brought back to Spain from the New World, or the Indies as it was referred to in the fifteenth century, Seville was then one of the richest and most active ports in Europe, a situation that lasted until the treacherous tides of the Guad-al-Quivir (Arabic for Great River) sunk so many treasure galleons arriving from their long and dangerous voyages from the New World that it seemed wiser to move the port to Cádiz. To make matters worse, the population of Seville was decimated by the plague known as the Black Death. Thereafter, Seville declined.

All the records of this great Age of Exploration are still contained in the city's Archivo General de Indias, nestled between the Cathedral and the Alcázar. Seville's large and dominating Gothic cathedral was the largest sanctuary in all of Europe until the building of St. Peter's in Rome and St. Paul's in London. It was built on the site of a Moorish mosque—which had itself been built upon Roman ruins. Its landmark tower, La Giralda (weathervane), the surviving minaret of the preexisting mosque, bears a close resemblance to the Koutoubia minaret in nearby Marrakech. And the Alcázar, a former Moorish palace, has been a royal residence continuously since the ninth century. Inside the Alcázar, we are instantly transported to Fez, thanks to the abundance of multicolored geometric tiles, panels of carved stucco with flowing Arab calligraphy, and coffered ceilings in gilded wood. This remarkable series of buildings and Moorish gardens represents a wonderful survey of Seville's architectural history, intermingling in a unique way Gothic, Renaissance, and Baroque styles as well as the rich Islamic architectural legacy of the eventually vanquished Moors.

In A.D. 711 Tarik, the governor of Tangiers, crossed the narrow straits separating Europe and Africa, conquered Tarifa and Gibraltar, and made his way north to Toledo, where his army fought against Don Roderigo in the battle of Guadalete. This

The courtyard of the Casa de Pilatos (above and opposite) is a remarkable combination of medieval, Gothic, Muslim, and Renaissance styles that could only have been created in southern Spain after the Moorish conquest in 711. The courtyard was one of the earliest parts of the Casa de Pilatos to be built, was enlarged, added to, and transformed over the centuries, the last touches being added by the Duchess of Denia in 1861. (Left) The main portal al'antica of the house, placed on a brick wall, is from the Genoa workshop of Antonio da Corona, and would be perfectly appropriate as the entrance of a Venetian palace.

was the beginning of what came to be known as "the reconquest" of Spain, a long struggle that lasted until late in the fifteenth century. Following a period of internecine struggle, al-Andalus, known today as Andalusia, became the most powerful kingdom in the Western world, and a place of great learning, beauty, and civilization. It was made up of many small states known as *taifas*, of which Seville was one. In the meanwhile, the various lands of northern Spain consolidated and Alfonso VI and other Spanish kings led a crusade against the Moors, in a struggle between Islamic and Christian forces for control of the Iberian peninsula. Seville became the capital of al-Andalus under a Berber dynasty, which built a great mosque there in 1184, and Andalusia became more and more a center of Islamic civilization. Over time, however, the Christian reconquest gained force. Isabella of Castille and Ferdinand of Aragon married in 1469, uniting the Christian kingdoms which mounted an offensive against the Nasrid kingdom, the last Muslim dynasty to rule in Spain. It fell in 1492, the year Christopher Columbus persuaded Queen Isabella to finance his expedition to what would be the New World. The Middle Ages came to an end and Spain entered its Golden Age.

The year 1492 also marked the death of Don Pedro Enriquez after he returned from the last battle to liberate Granada, in which he had participated with his sons. As an uncle of the Catholic king, royal blood flowed in the veins of Don Pedro, who first married Doña Beatriz de Ribera, the Countess of Molarés, who gave him two male heirs, Fernando and Fadrique, before she died in 1470. He then married her sister, the extremely rich Doña Catalina de Ribera. It was Don Pedro who gave birth to the Casa de Pilatos in September 1483 when he was Provincial Governor of Andalusia, by buying some houses in Seville's San Esteban district, in the very heart of the old city. These had been confiscated from a heretic by the Inquisition, and were on the Calle Real, the old royal road which became the Calle Imperial after Charles V used it to enter Seville to marry Isabella of Portugal in the Alcázar.

Don Pedro paid a high price for the houses since valuable water rights—normally reserved for the Alcázar and a few convents—went with them. This was particularly important in Seville, where Islamic buildings needed a lot of water for their fountains and gardens. The Enriquez de Riberas moved out of their old house in the Calle San Luis and into their new house, which they called the Palacio Nuevo. Don Pedro's brother lived nearby, which was useful as clans then gathered together to fight off marauders and robbers. With this house, Don Pedro was making a statement about his new and rich family dynasty. Thanks to his second marriage, he also obtained the right for him and his family to be buried in the prestigious crypt of the Gothic-Mudéjar chapel in the Cartuja de Santa María de las Cuevas, where he created an important family mausoleum. He soon proceeded to buy other houses adjacent

(Opposite) The marble fountain in the courtyard is upheld by three dolphins and crowned by the three heads of the god Janus. The fountain was commissioned in 1529 from the Aprile bottegha in Naples by Don Fadrique de Ribera, the first Duke of Tarifa, and the first family member to travel extensively in Europe. He was immensely rich, became totally infatuated with Renaissance art while in Italy, and ordered two tombs for his parents from the studio of Gaggia and Bissone in Genoa. These were the first Italian Renaissance pieces to arrive in Seville and made a major impact. Don Fadrique traveled as far as Jerusalem, where he visited Pontius Pilate's house and conceived the idea of linking his Seville palace to the Stations of the Cross. (Above) A sculpture of Pallas Athena dated 52 BC joins thirteen Italian Renaissance columns, also purchased by Don Fadrique.

to those with which he began. The process was rather like assembling a mosaic and went on through several generations, each generation acquiring more houses, which they reshaped, redesigned, and redecorated. Together the family created the most spectacular and beautiful courtyard in southern Spain (pages 28–33), a dazzling series of rooms clad in Islamic tiles with brilliantly colored calligraphic inscriptions (pages 34, 35), Renaissance loggias and galleries where the family kept a renowned collection of antique sculpture, gardens to take one's breath away, and a series of rooms of state in which the family treasures—tapestries, old master paintings, silver and gold objects—were very much at home. They carved out a large plaza outside the house, and at one time owned and rented out all the houses on it. To their own palace they added a second-storey Renaissance loggia from which they could watch bullfights and other spectacles. The plaza was embellished in the early twentieth century with a bronze statue of Francisco de Zurbarán holding his paint brushes, possibly about to go to work on the large, multipaneled altarpiece in the adjacent Church of San Esteban.

Much of the history of this great house is still steeped in legend, hearsay, and folklore. To figure out which family members did what, scholars must go into the vast family archives

Moorish tiles were used extensively in the Casa de Pilatos, and make an opulent and unusual background for Renaissance and Gothic architecture or Roman antiquities. (Opposite) A remarkable staircase leading to the first floor of the house. It is crowned by a richly carved, Moorish, gilded-wood dome with family arms supported by escutcheons painted by Andrés Pérez in 1537. Embedded in a wall is a niche that, according to legend, once held the ashes of Pontius Pilate and is marked with a representation of the cock that crowed when St. Peter denied Jesus for the third time. (Above) The Pretorian Hall contains typical, carved Arabic doors, richly colored tiled walls—into which are set the coats of arms of the Enriquez, Ribera, and other families linked to the house—and carved plaster with Islamic calligraphy.

kept in the house, which are now curated by the Medinaceli Foundation. The latest such effort was made by Professor Vincente Lleo Canal, whose delightful and scholarly book, *La Casa de Pilatos*, is the basis of much of the information to follow. Despite contradictory accounts of the development of the house, we are sure that Don Pedro was responsible for the small chapel off the main courtyard, thanks to its Gothic vaults and an Arabic inscription on the stucco-filled walls reading, "For our Lord and Master Don Pedro, may he be exalted;" and we must assume that he also created the Mudéjar-Gothic-Moorish courtyard—albeit of smaller dimensions than the one that exists today. The courtyard in its present state includes later Renaissance additions and even Gothic Revival embellishments added by the Duchess of Denia in 1861. Don Pedro also created a series of small rooms for the servants and family as well as larger reception rooms that suited the family's dignity and functions. The archives tell us that ninety-two servants lived in the house, including plasterers, carpenters, stable boys, and so on. We may assume that most of their rooms were on the ground floor, as was the custom. And at one time a group of scholars, musicians, and humanists also lived there.

After Don Pedro died and following the death of his older son, Don Fernando, in 1509, the younger son, Don Fadrique, received the family titles, honors, and fortune. By then, Seville was in full glory and considered a second Rome. The city's horizons expanded, its noblemen started traveling abroad where they were particularly impressed with Renaissance Italy, whose ideas, art, and architecture they brought home and, in turn, exported to the New World. Don Fadrique was more sophisticated than his late father, and in 1514 received the title of the Marquis of Tarifa from Queen Juana, who also made him *Notario Mayor* of Seville in 1539. Don Fadrique's vast fortune consisted of millions inherited from his mother in property, and the soap monopoly that King Juan II had given the family in 1423. He had received a modern education with heavy emphasis on the classics and built up what was then considered a large library of eight thousand books, including works by Dante, Petrarch, and Erasmus, books on Rome, Marco Polo's travels, and the writings of Caesar, Seneca, and Joseph Flavius. In the years 1518 to 1520 he traveled through Europe with an entourage of twelve servants, finally ending up in Jerusalem. There he visited what was purported to have been the house of Pontius Pilate, the Roman governor. The marquis measured the distance from Pilate's house to Golgotha and realized that it was exactly the same distance as that between his house in Seville and a cross standing in a field in the countryside, known as the Cruz del Campo. Don Fadrique thereafter made his house the first stop on his own Via Dolorosa. He would mark out the various stages in different parts of the city, and the Nuevo Palacio became known as the Casa de Pilatos.

The Jàrdin Grande (preceding pages and this page), originally known as the kitchen garden, is a large, heavily planted area of formal gardens at one end of the house, its greenery highlighted by bright bougainvillea and ripe oranges. It dates from the time of Don Fadrique and was altered between 1568–1570 by the Italian architect Benvenuto Tortello. He built here two identical sections of superimposed loggias with arches resting on old marble columns. (Opposite) A terrace overlooking the garden, where the present Duchess of Medinaceli, head of the house, likes to have a sherry and tapas before lunch. The carafe and glasses bear the family crown.

The Járdin Chico, or small garden (above) is placed in front of the Zaquizami Corridor, where some of the antiquities purchased by Per Afán de Ribera, the heir of Don Fadrique, are displayed. Per Afán was made Viceroy of Naples, the most important post that could be obtained outside Spain. While there, he amassed a great collection of antiquities, comparable only to those of Cosimo de Medici and Cardinal Farnese. He shipped the collection to Spain. Some pieces were lost to pirates, others in shipwrecks, but most arrived safely and were placed in especially made galleries adjacent to the garden (left and opposite), in niches on the garden side, and in roundels in the Patio Grande. A nymph sleeps quietly on a warm spring day on a ledge of one of the galleries, protected from the elements by a richly carved, gilded Islamic ceiling.

A glass door of the Salon de los Frescos (above), that originally contained stained glass panels, opens on to the first floor terrace. This is one of several reception rooms principally used in the cooler months of the year that were created in the sixteenth century to enhance the importance of the Enriquez de Ribera family. Most of the downstairs rooms are open to the elements, and ideal for entertaining in the mostly clement weather that prevails in southern Spain. The Salon (opposite) was recently renamed after the discovery of a series of murals of 1539, depicting the Triumph of the Seasons by Arnao de Vergara. This was one of the rooms and terraces used to film Lawrence of Arabia with Peter O'Toole. On display are several Roman busts.

He also traveled widely throughout Italy, visiting Lombardy, Venice, Florence, Rome, and Naples, and was particularly impressed with the Duomo in Milan and the nearby Certosa in Pavia, the latter inspiring him to commission in 1520 two classical marble tombs for his parents from the studio of Gaggia and Bissone in Genoa. He sent two sculptors from the workshop to Seville to install the tombs in the family sepulcher. These were among the first Italian Renaissance works of art seen in Seville and made a major impact. In 1528 he also ordered an Italian portal *al'antica* from Antonio da Carona for the main entrance of the Casa de Pilatos, and this was applied to the brick facade of the house—and may well lead a visitor to wonder if he will be entering a Moorish Casbah or an Italian palazzo. Corinthian pilasters, red marble roundels, and relief portraits of emperors are crowned by three Jerusalem crosses, signifying the house's new identity.

He also bought additional houses and land to increase the acreage of the Casa de Pilatos by half, and that included space for what became known as the Great Garden. The garden is framed by three loggias with arches embellished with reliefs of emperors inspired by the Medici villa Poggio a Caiano near Rome. A corridor leads to two Italianate galleries (with a touch of Islamic calligraphy) for exhibiting antiquities. We also assume that Don Fadrique decorated a whole series of rooms between the patio and the chapel, which were christened with names relating to Pontius Pilate's life. These rooms are paved with Islamic tiles bearing the Enriquez and de Ribera coats of arms, and they have traditional Moorish carved-wood ceilings as well as Arabic inscriptions in stucco. Don Fadrique also expanded and "modernized" the central patio built by his father, bringing the Italian Renaissance to the Gothic-Moorish courtyard. And it was here that Don Fadrique placed thirteen marble columns he had purchased in Genoa; this courtyard was subsequently to be filled with antiquities collected by the next head of the house, the first Duke of Alcalá. Don Fadrique also commissioned the exceptionally fine and elaborate Moorish tile-clad staircase (page 34) that leads to the first floor, which he also considerably expanded. The first-floor rooms were mostly used in winter and those on the ground floor during the summer since they gave onto the garden and patio. The ground floor was considered rather public while the first floor was designed as a private and more exclusive reception area of the house. The carved ceiling crowning the staircase is the most beautiful in the palace, and embedded in the walls is a small niche with an effigy of the rooster that crowed when Christ died, and is said to have once contained the ashes of Pontius Pilate.

Don Fadrique also built a *guardaroba* that housed his art collection, books, and other treasures, rather like the *wunderkammern* or *kunstkammern* of northern Europe. His treasures included medallions, engraved gems, pieces in gold and silver, and a Byzantine icon. There were also "bedroom decorations" that

included 230 tapestries from Tournai, Flanders, and Arras, as well as many precious Oriental carpets, and also collections of musical instruments and paintings. Many of these objects, along with furniture in Córdoba leather, were spread through the house creating a sumptuous decoration worthy of a humanist and man of letters.

Don Fadrique's heir was his nephew Per Afán de Ribera, a politician and diplomat, who had gained his uncle's enmity when he divorced his first wife, Leonor Ponce de Léon, the Marchioness of Zahara, and daughter of the discoverer of Florida. The divorce also elicited an unfavorable reaction from king Felipe II who, notwithstanding, made him Viceroy of Catalonia between 1554 and 1558, and then made him Viceroy of Naples, Spain's most important post abroad. While in Naples, he commissioned an important fountain from the sculptors Giovan Domenico d'Auria and Annibale Caccavello; the latter also advised Per Afán on his highly important collection of antiquities—a collection comparable to those amassed by the popes, Cosimo de Medici, and Cardinal Farnese. In due course, the collection was shipped to Seville, though many pieces were lost to pirates and storms on the way. Among his most famous purchases were a Venus attributed to Praxiteles and a large statue of Pallas Athena ascribed to Agorakritos of

Paros (pages 32, 33), and these still stand in the courtyard. Per Afán brought the Neapolitan architect Benvenuto Tortello to Seville to install his sculpture in a contemporary fashion and to transform the medieval rooms into "modern" apartments. His many busts of Roman emperors and one of Charles V were placed in specially designed round niches along the central patio. Other portraits were placed above the arches of the loggias. Some statues were ancient, some Roman copies, some contemporary, and the collection was world famous in its time. It is difficult to appraise its quality today since much of it was later sent to the Medinaceli Palace in Madrid or sold. What has remained lends immense charm and unique character to the Casa de Pilatos.

Per Afán's projects were mainly in the area of the Great Garden, which fully bears his imprint, and he expanded the *guardaroba* to contain his many purchases. Per Afán died heirless in Naples in 1571 (although he had several illegitimate children, including the saint Juan de Ribera), and so his younger brother Don Fernando Enriquez de Ribera succeeded him. This third duke, who had married the daughter of the conqueror of Mexico, Hernando Cortés, had his own palace (the Palacio de Dueñas, which now belongs to the Duchess of Alba), and didn't want to move over to Pilatos, and so rented

The library (left) contains an infinitesimal part of the books that were once in the family collections. Don Fadrique built up a famous library during his lifetime, reputed to be more important than that of Oxford University at the time. And he had several writers living in the house, as a sort of resident academy. Today, a large area of the house is devoted to the archives of the Medinaceli family, and contains over a million documents covering a thousand years of family history. The Salon de Pacheco (below) was named after Francisco Pacheco, Velázquez's father-in-law who painted The Triumph of Hercules and other mythological scenes on the ceiling. This salon, like the others, is heated in winter by Arabic braziers (opposite).

it out in 1587. Don Fernando spent nothing on Pilatos and died in 1590, leaving the house to his seven-year-old son, also called Fernando, who would marry at the early age of fourteen. In 1594, young Fernando and his mother moved back into the Casa de Pilatos where, later in life, he set up a rather famous salon, or academy, a place where humanists, historians, and other scholars gathered. This third Duke of Alcalá had a brilliant political life due to his place in the inner circle of King Felipe IV, who appointed him Governor of Milan in 1627, and Viceroy of Naples in 1630—the second member of the family to have this important and prestigious position. He was so useful to the king in Naples and other cities abroad, that he never returned to Seville to live and, as a consequence, did little to change the house. Living in Italy and traveling in Europe, on the other hand, allowed him to collect on a scale that would have been impossible had he remained in Spain, and this is reflected in an inventory of the collections which he ordered in 1637 while in Naples.

The third Duke of Alcalá decorated several rooms on the first floor—rooms in which would hang many of the paintings he acquired abroad. His most important commission was for a ceiling by the painter Francisco Pacheco, the subject of which was an homage to the duke in mythological terms. Reading the 1637 inventory, there is an impressive list of works, including paintings by Titian, Dürer, Michelangelo, Ribera, and Raphael, as well as fourteen Venetian portraits. It is certain that some of these works were studio or second versions or contemporary copies. But we are certainly curious to know more about the *Sacrifice of Abraham* attributed to Andrea del Sarto, or the *Holy Family* given to Tintoretto, or the two philosophers by Ribera. We read in the inventory that the perplexing portrait of a bearded lady by José de Ribera, which is today—along with other paintings that remained in the family collection—in the Palácio de Tavera in Toledo (another palace belonging to the family), had now entered the collection. In the inventory, there is also mention of many small bronzes, several by Giambologna, and the sort of jeweled objects that were typically found in other royal and princely *schatzkammern*. And the inventory mentions a great many seventeenth-century Spanish works, including several that are now elsewhere. Unfortunately, the ninth Duke of Medinaceli gave Velázquez's masterpiece, *The Weavers*, to King Felipe V. The painting can today be seen at the Prado. Of the 325 paintings mentioned in the inventory, only fifty-four can be definitively identified, but these alone are enough to have made the collection of the Casa de Pilatos the equal of many of Europe's finest.

The Enriquez de Riberas were, quite obviously, people of great accomplishment, taste, culture, and wealth. But they were cursed with a lack of male heirs, which meant that many branches died out and that their fortunes and titles passed outside the direct line of succession. Today, these are all invested in the Dukes of Medinaceli, one of Spain's noblest

and richest families, also from Seville. Tracing the lineage of the Royal House of Medinaceli from the thirteenth century to the present through its different lines—the kings of France and Castile, the Royal House of La Cerda, the de Ribera, Enriquez, and Cogolludo dynasties—is a task best left to the genealogists. The Medinaceli family, who possessed a great many properties, decided not to live in the Casa de Pilatos as of 1658, and it fell into disrepair. Some rooms were made into offices, others were closed up, and the employees who remained to take care of the house had to move out of their own rooms to make way for the Medinacelis when they came to visit once a year. Many of the house's treasures were sent to the family's palace in Madrid, which was sold in the late nineteenth century when the Medinacelis moved to an equally large but more modern house in the nearby Plaza Colon. The old palace became the Palace Hotel, although the family kept the chapel. They had employed close to three thousand servants in Madrid before the move, and that must have been a bit onerous even for them!

The present Duchess of Medinaceli, Victoria Eugenia (known to her bridge partners as Mimi), is the head of 120 different families, bears fifty-two titles (of which nine have been distributed among her children), and her oldest son, the Marques de

The Eastern Portrait Room (opposite) is centered on a large painting by Sotomayor of the mother of the present Duchess of Medinaceli. In the portrait she is dressed for a royal reception at her Madrid Palace. The Medinacelis were a kingdom within the Kingdom, and very close to the Spanish Royal Family. The present duchess, Victoria Eugenia, went into exile when the Republic was declared on the same train as the Queen of Spain and then returned to Seville during the civil war. Draped over the canapé is her wedding dress (opposite). Her photograph as a young woman (right) at the Feria, an annual event that takes place immediately after Holy Week, shows her in the traditional mantilla worn by Sevillianas. Draped over a Napoleon III settee in the upstairs study (above), is one of the duchess's many fans and capes. Hanging next to the fireplace is a view of Naples by Vanvitelli, part of the renowned family painting collection, most of which is now in a museum in Toledo run by the family foundation.

Afternoon tea is set in front of the fireplace in the dining room (opposite), a long, stately chamber that has a table for twenty-four. The fireplace used to be in the library, and above it is a 1679 still life by the Neapolitan painter Giuseppe Recco. The doors and windows are framed by friezes of Islamic calligraphy and have shutters to keep out the intense summer sun. (Above) The Medinaceli arms on the family silver and tea service. (Previous pages) In the duchess's living room are family photographs and some of the cups she won at bridge tournament.

Cogolludo, will be the next head of the family. The Medinacelis were once, in effect, a state within the kingdom, and their land holdings, according to Mimi's third son Ignacio, the Duke of Segorbe, were larger than the territories of such Italian duchies as Milan, Parma, or Ferrara, and possibly larger than that of the Venetian Republic at the height of its powers.

The present duchess, the eighteenth to bear the title, was born in Madrid and left Spain after King Alfonso XIII chose exile in 1931 upon the proclamation of the Second Spanish Republic. But she returned to live in the Casa de Pilatos during the Spanish Civil War, met and married Rafael de Medina in Seville, and passed her title to him as allowed by Spanish law. The Duchess and her children made their home at the Casa de Pilatos, and slowly worked to bring the house back to life. Although parts of the house and grounds are now open to visitors, the Duchess still lives there year round in a private wing filled with photographs of family and friends (pages 48, 49), portraits of herself by Sorolla, family souvenirs, and her personal collection of porcelain piglets.

In recent years the Duke of Segorbe convinced his mother and his siblings to transfer ownership of their many family properties, including the Casa de Pilatos, to a foundation called the Fundación Casa Ducal de Medinaceli. This move allowed the family to keep its vast properties together—rather than seeing them divided up among various branches of the family—as well as to manage them more effectively. Don Ignacio claims the Foundation is responsible for the upkeep of eighty-six thousand acres of roof! Other properties now managed by the Foundation include the Palacio de Tavera in Toledo, an archive of the Spanish nobility where they keep their works of art, Pazo de Oca near Santiago de Compostela, one of the most beautiful gardens in Spain, the Palacio Medinaceli in Soria, two hours from Madrid, the Palacio de Cogolludo near Guadalajara, as well as many smaller houses.

The Duchess of Medinaceli and the Segorbes still entertain their friends at the ancestral home in Seville. On such occasions they will place family treasures back in the now public salons, and fill them with roses from the country. One of the most beautiful parties celebrated the fiftieth birthday of Prince Michael of Greece; people danced in the Moorish courtyard, listened to flamenco in tiled rooms off the garden, and dined in the fragrant garden. During hours when the house is open to the public, Mimi—who speaks the perfect, clipped English of a British chatelaine and the French last used in Proust's salons in the Faubourg St. Germain—enjoys walking in her gardens, chatting up tourists, and then surprising them by revealing who she is.

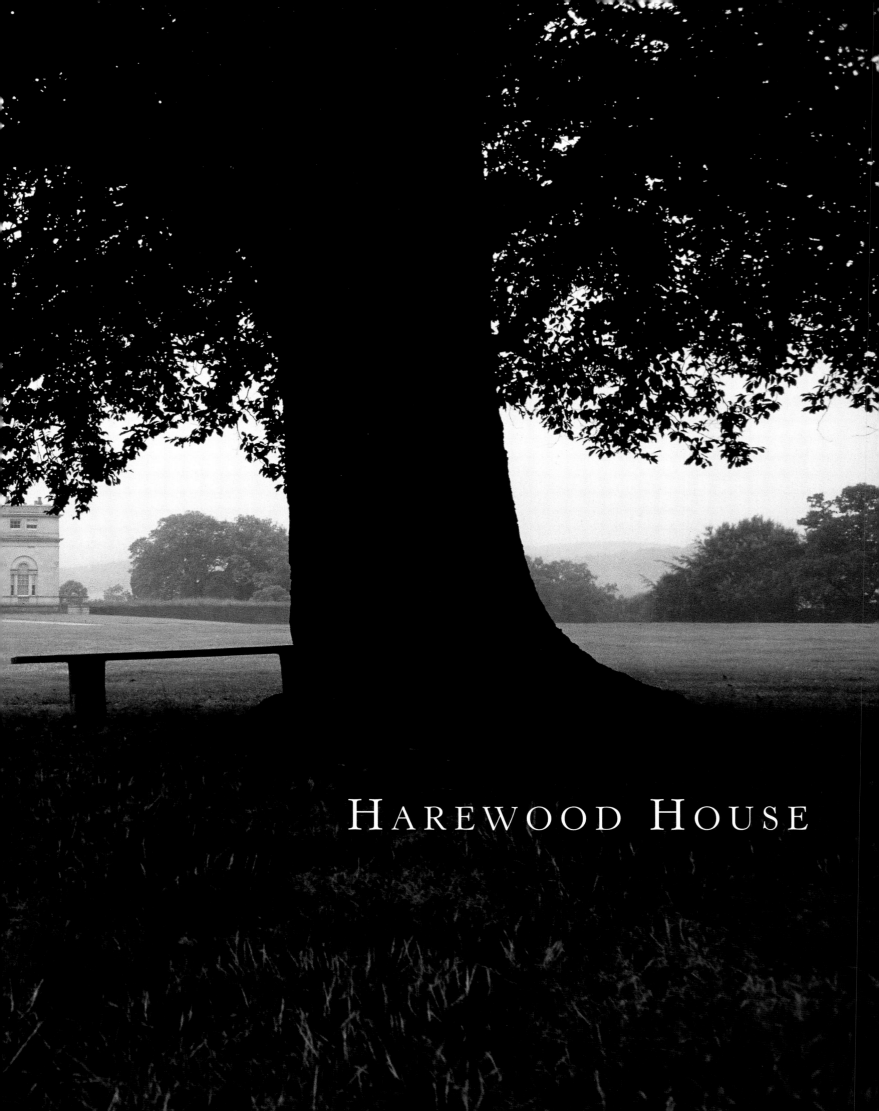

HAREWOOD HOUSE

The Best of Robert Adam, Capability Brown, and Thomas Chippendale

In 1922, Henry Viscount Lascelles, who was to become the sixth Earl of Harewood in 1929, married Princess Mary, the only daughter of George V and the sister of two British monarchs, Edward VIII and George VI. In 1930, the King bestowed upon his daughter the title of HRH The Princess Royal, and, at the appropriate time, he and Queen Mary had looked around to find her a husband. Before World War I, such marriages were generally contracted with German princelings, but the prevailing anti-German sentiment changed all that, and so the British Royal Family looked to an alliance with one of their own. Henry Viscount Lascelles, known as Harry, was a highly eligible bachelor. In 1917, he was made immensely rich by an unexpected inheritance from a great uncle. He was elegant, very British, and destined to inherit a renowned country house with a great art collection and a London town house in Mayfair, and he was to live in the Jacobean Goldsborough Hall, the Yorkshire estate that was used by the eldest Lascelles son. Harry was the perfect consort for a royal princess, and his principal residence, Harewood House, would be a suitable setting for a king's daughter.

Harewood is among the most interesting of English country houses and it bears the mark of Robert Adam, Charles Carr, Capability Brown, Thomas Chippendale, and Sir Charles Barry. There was a grand wedding at Westminster Abbey on February 28, 1922, and the young couple lost no time in giving birth to their son and heir George in 1923, and to Gerald, their spare, the following year. In 1929, the fifth earl died, and the next year Harry, the Princess Royal, George, and Gerald moved into Harewood House, where they enjoyed a close family life. Both the royal standard and the Lascelles flag flew over the house and George V and Queen Mary were frequent visitors. When war was declared in 1939, the handsome George Lascelles (page 60) joined the Grenadier Guards. He was severely wounded in Italy when a bullet missed his heart by a few centimeters, and he was subsequently captured by the Nazis. During his imprisonment in Colditz Castle, he developed a passion for classical music. Shortly after the war, the young Viscount Lascelles became the seventh Earl of Harewood, and he began his career as an opera reviewer for *Ballet* magazine. He then became editor of *Opera* magazine, and he was soon appointed a director of the Royal Opera House, Covent Garden. The renowned conductor and musical director, Sir George Solti, wrote of Harewood in his memoirs, "He has a greater knowledge of musical matters and usage than anyone I have come across in an opera house." Lord Harewood was a close friend and collaborator of Benjamin

Visitors enter the Harewood property through a large classical archway (above) built in 1901–1903. A road through the lovely English park leads the visitor through the property (right), and the first building they come upon is the small All Saints Church that was built in 1410 for the granddaughters of William Lord Alburgh, who erected a castle nearby in 1367. The church contains six remarkable tombs of deceased family members executed 1419–1510 (opposite). The neo-Palladian façade of the new house built as of 1759 by Edwin Lascelles, (previous pages) is best seen from a bench near an ancient elm near the entrance to the church.

The southern façade of the house (opposite) overlooks an essentially man-made landscape, one of whose main features is a large artificial lake created by Capability Brown seen (above) in a photograph of 1860 by Roger Fenton. Lady Louisa Thynne, wife of the third Earl of Harewood, hired Sir Charles Barry, architect of the Houses of Parliament, to remodel Harewood's eighteenth-century house and gardens to conform to the life style of the Victorian period, and one of his main contributions was this immense, multi-tiered terrace.

The lower terrace (overleaf), the one we see in Fenton's photograph, is a sumptuous French garden parterre with stone fountains, urns, and statuary, while one of the upper terraces (opposite) has become an English flowered border. A narrow terrace also runs around the south façade and has often been used by Lascelles youngsters for bicycle rides, particularly after a Sunday lunch (above).

Britten and together they created *Gloriana*, an opera to celebrate the Coronation of Harewood's cousin, Queen Elizabeth II. In 1956, Lord Harewood cofounded the English Stage Company with George Devine and Ronald Duncan, starting out with a production of John Osborne's *Look Back in Anger*. In the 1970s, after a stint at the Edinburgh Festival, he moved on to become Director and later Chairman of the board of the English National Opera, housed at the Coliseum Theatre. The ENO is a swinging answer to the more staid and traditional Covent Garden, and Harewood developed new, young audiences thanks to such exciting directors as Jonathan Miller and David Pountney and singers like Josephine Barstow.

George Harewood has quietly followed his own star. The Duke of Windsor (formerly Edward VIII) saw his nephew's talent in a somewhat different way. "It's very odd about George and music," he liked to say. "You know, his parents were quite normal—liked horses and dogs and the country." However, Harewood did have his share of press attention when he was divorced from his first wife Marion Stein and married Patricia Tuckwell, a beautiful model and violinist in the Sydney Symphony (page 64). This has been a particularly happy and fruitful union with a great many common interests: art, music, intelligent and talented friends. These are reflected in the cozy, flower-filled sitting room that looks out over the Terrace (page 65) at Harewood. It is full of works of art that they have collected together, including paintings by Australian artists Sidney Nolan and Arthur Boyd, drawings of the Harewoods by David Hankinson, an Egon Schiele portrait of Arnold Schoenberg, Walter Sickert paintings from the Camden Town Murder series and his portrait of the singer Mattia Battistini, as well as a bronze statuette by Henri Gaudier-Brzeska of Bolm and Karsavina dancing Stravinsky's "Firebird."

George and Patricia have guided the destiny of Harewood House through periods of high taxation, ever-growing expenses, and ongoing programs of restoration and redecoration. Owing to their vision, the large house has never been in better shape. The State Apartments were opened to the public on a permanent basis in 1950, more rooms were opened in 1957, and amenities for visitors were provided. After the death

This is one of three libraries at Harewood, but the only one untouched by Barry's nineteenth-century alterations. Adam's neoclassical hand is evident in the Corinthian columns and elaborate stucco ceiling. The Library, completed in the 1760s, contained over 4,000 books and has served as a civilized place to read, work, play chess, and talk by the fire. Recessed arches with busts of Petrarch, Boccacio, Macchiavelli, Dante, and Isaac Newton (opposite) set the mood for discussing important issues on an elevated plane, conversations that were part and parcel of weekends in England's country houses. Statesmen, industrialists, bankers, and peers of the realm met at Harewood to formulate the nation's policies. George Lascelles (above) as a young man radiates the confidence of his age.

of the Princess Royal in 1965, the entire East Wing was also opened up. Receiving visitors was nothing new, since Harewood housekeepers had always shown interested and well-behaved visitors through the main reception rooms by appointment, and this is clear from guide books published in the nineteenth century.

For several reasons, Harewood House soon became one of the most popular stately homes in Britain. There is no house where the neoclassical, Greek Revival style of Adam and Chippendale can be so intensely felt, and yet the house has a lived-in feeling despite the opulence of its decoration and its priceless collections. Also, people are impressed by the royal connection. The tabletops are filled with photographs of Harewood house parties of Edwardian ladies and gentlemen dressed to the nines on a hot summer afternoon, and semi-formal snapshots of various kings and emperors in their admiral's caps on royal yachts, sporting the neatly trimmed beards that enforce the family resemblance.

Even though the Harewoods now live upstairs, they entertain their guests in the formal rooms downstairs when they so choose, although they seldom do. When the house is closed to visitors at Christmas, the family still gathers in the Library (page 75). This room was once referred to as the Saloon, and it is in fact still more a sitting room than a reading room, but it gets its name from the nineteenth-century addition of large mahogany bookshelves by Sir Charles Barry, the architect of the Houses of Parliament, who remodeled the house in the 1840s. George Harewood remembers driving over from Goldsbourough Hall nearly seventy-five years ago to spend Christmas with his grandparents, where young and old family members gathered in the Library to await the arrival of Father Christmas. Great palm trees filled the corners of this large room where antimacassars lay on the backs of most of the chairs and children played bagatelle before moving on to the vast formal dining room, and looked forward to being offered one chocolate after lunch. This room, says Harewood, "began gradually in my subconscious mind to assume the position its chosen refuge does to an animal, and became the room that for me most embodied home." Once Harewood moved into the house, after the death of his father, it remained the place where everybody got together "to talk racing and cricket and music, read newspapers or listen to the radio when we weren't busying ourselves with something more active." Such activities included riding bicycles around the Terrace (page 56), taking long walks through the snow in the game-filled forest, or driving to nearby Leeds or Harrogate to buy a book or record. When he now gathers his large family in the same room at Christmas, he wonders "if my own grandchildren, as they play games or make confetti of the wrappings of their Christmas presents, are developing an affection for the Library as I did at their age."

The answer is, of course, a resounding yes. And this affection, even passion, for Harewood House began in 1759 with George Harewood's ancestor Edwin Lascelles, who laid the foundation stone in that year. Edwin's father, Henry, came from a well-established Yorkshire family, and purchased two adjoining estates, Gawthorp and Harewood, in the West Riding of Yorkshire in 1739. He was quite fortunate to be able to do so since estates of such size seldom came up for sale. The property was not far from Leeds, which was to become an important industrial center, or from York, the major city of North England, with its magnificent cathedral, and a place where diversion and society could be found. To possess such an estate was to have attained social and political power.

Henry Lascelles had founded Lascelles and Maxwell, a London trading house that profited from customs concessions, government contracts, and the exportation of sugar from Barbados in the West Indies. The firm extended credit to farmers and planters, and brought in slaves from Africa to cut and process the cane to make the sugar that sweetened newly fashionable coffee and chocolate and was essential for making rum. Sugar beet farming had not yet started in Europe, so the West Indies planters enjoyed a highly profitable business. But when plantation owners had a bit of bad luck or overproduced

The Princess Royal's marriage to Henry Lascelles transformed Harewood from a great country house to a royal residence. The daughter of King George V, she is seen (above left) holding her new born son, George, who became the seventh Earl of Harewood, pictured a few years later (left) with his brother Gerald dressed in kilts on the occasion of George V's Silver Jubilee in 1935. A small wing was designed for the princess at Harewood by Sir Herbert Baker, Lutyen's associate in New Delhi, (above and overleaf top) which had a charming marble and silver bathroom. When the Princess Royal and the new earl moved to Harewood in 1929, the earl occupied an Adam bedroom in the East Wing (opposite) that contained an exceptional set of green lacquer Chinoiserie furniture made by Thomas Chippendale. On the earl's desk are family photographs and, as he worked here, he enjoyed a view of Wharfdale.

and the price of sugar crashed, they defaulted on their loans and Lascelles and Maxwell took over their farms, becoming in the process the largest and richest landowners in the West Indies. In 1755, Edwin Lascelles made a trial run for his house-to-be by building rather imposing stables to the west of Old Gawthorp Hall. He selected two respected Yorkshire architects, brothers John and Robert Carr, to supervise the work. John Carr had worked for Lord Burlington, a pioneer of Palladianism, and quickly earned the full confidence of Lascelles. Notwithstanding, Lascelles was also considering Sir William Chambers, one of the leading exponents of the Palladian style in England who had written the respected *Treatise on the Decorative Part of Civil Architecture*. Like most young English gentlemen, Chambers had gone on the Grand Tour, a civilizing peregrination across the Alps to discover the art and architecture of antiquity as well as the wonders of Renaissance Italy. Young gentlemen, often in the company of a tutor, known as "a bear," all passed through Venice, where many lost their virginity in the city's *ridotti*, and they visited Vicenza and the Veneto, with its beautiful villas designed by Andrea Palladio, before proceeding to Florence and Rome. Chambers actually studied architecture in both Paris and Rome, returning to England in 1755 after a six-year learning process. A Yorkshire friend recommended that he make drawings for Lascelles' new house in the Palladian style, which was then the rage, warning that "he has had plans from everybody in England" and that "you be upon your guard to submit as compleat a design as you are able." Chambers soon did so, and Lascelles sent him a hundred pounds for his trouble. Lascelles then forwarded the plans to Lord Leicester, who had just built Holkham Hall, his own Palladian house decorated by Robert Adam. After several months Lascelles informed Chambers that his plans had been refused.

Leicester also reviewed Carr's plans for Harewood House, and in March 1758 Lascelles made motions to settle on a price for the work, asking Carr when he would next be in London. Apparently Capability Brown, who was later commissioned to landscape the grounds, had also been approached to make a set of plans, and in June of 1758, Lady Lindores added to the possibilities when she introduced Robert Adam to Lascelles. Adam had made the Grand Tour on the continent, had studied the Roman ruins, collected antiquities, and developed the design vocabulary and very personal style that he expressed at Harewood House and elsewhere, and which was to make such a major impact on the history of British architecture. He mastered a vast array of antique forms and ornament, inspired by what he called the "gaiety" of interior decoration at the Baths of Diocletian and Caracalla and the recent excavations at Herculaneum and Pompeii, and he took up the grotesquerie he saw in the Vatican Loggie and in such Renaissance palaces as the Villa Madama and Villa Caparola. All this was expressed in the brilliant palette he used to color his elaborate

The present Earl of Harewood enjoyed a brilliant musical career at Covent Garden, the English National Opera, and as Artistic Director of the Edinburgh, Leeds, and Adelaide Festivals. He is seen (left) with his second wife Patricia Tuckwell, a flautist in the Adelaide Symphony, and the lutenist Julian Bream. George Harewood's study (opposite) is filled with memorabilia of his musical career, including a portrait of the Viennese composer Arnold Schoenberg, a drawing of the Italian singer Mattia Battistini, a bust of Maria Callas, with whom he worked very closely, and a watercolor of the conductor Karl Böhm. The Harewoods are serious collectors of modern art, and seen here are works by Egon Schiele, Jacob Epstein, Francis Bacon, Sidney Nolan, Walter Sickert, and Pablo Picasso. Lord Harewood's music archives are in the nearby Leeds Library.

stucco work, including pinks and greens, pale turquoise and vermilion, Wedgwood grays, and a great deal of gold high-lighting.

Adam, like Chambers, had recently returned from Italy, so Lascelles asked Adam to critique Carr's Palladian elevations and plans and make some suggestions. Adam found it difficult to comply. "I have made some Alterations on it," he wrote to his brother James, "but as the plan did not admit of a great many, that has prevented the fronts from being Changed like-wise." He was rather eager to be employed because the rejected Chambers was his major competitor. Adam did come up with one genial change to the plans, which consisted of two semicircular back courts between the house and wings. One of the courts was rejected by Lascelles and the other disappeared during the nineteenth-century reconstruction. Adam made some minor changes to Carr's somewhat stereotypical Palladian facade, and Carr's interior design was chosen for the family rooms on the east side of the house while Adam's design was adopted for the State Apartments on the west side. Adam was paid a large fee for his suggestions and hired as interior decorator for the entire project. This was not an uncommon arrangement, since Adam decorated many a house for which other architects had made the plans. Due to

Louis XIV started the fashion for state bedrooms at Versailles, and they were soon an essential element of royal palaces and stately homes. The State Bedroom at Harewood was designed by Adam and probably used as such only by the visiting Duchess of Kent and her daughter Victoria as well as Grand Duke Nicholas of Russia, who came to the house in 1816. The magnificent carved giltwood bed was delivered by Chippendale in 1772 for a total cost of 400 pounds, making it one of his most expensive pieces of furniture. For this room, he also supplied black and lacquered gold furniture and two elaborate gilt mirrors.

When Harewood was reconfigured by Charles Barry in the 1840s, all this furniture was packed up in crates and the State Bedroom became a comfortable sitting room. The crates were forgotten and only rediscovered in the 1970s, when the bedroom reassumed its original character. It now contains Chippendale's masterpiece, the Diana and Minerva satinwood commode (above) with marqueterie and ivory inlays. Above the commode is a portrait of Mrs. Scott and her daughter Henrietta by Richard Crossway and opposite, over the fireplace, is a portrait of Viscount Lascelles by John Hoppner. (Overleaf left) A Sèvres biscuit group offered to Edwin Lascelles and the Princess Royal as a wedding gift from the city of Paris.

(Preceding pages, above) The silk for the Yellow Drawing Room was chosen by Edwin Lascelles after Adam had painted the stucco ceiling. The rococo gilded mirrors, the carved white marble fireplace, the refined curvilinear furniture highlighted in a second color, and the decorative carpet were all designed by Adam. This sumptuous and harmonious ensemble fully explains why Adam was the most sought-after decorator of his time in England. On the right of the fireplace is a portrait of the renowned singer Adelina Patti by Franz Winterhalter, and on the left is a Harewood family relative, Mrs. Harding, by Sir Joshua Reynolds.

(Opposite) The Cinnamon Drawing Room started out as a dining room. It then became a sitting room intended for a set of important Gobelin tapestries that Edwin Lascelles had discovered in Paris in 1756. The tapestries were never purchased, however, and the walls were upholstered in white silk. In 1989, many of the great family portraits in the house were transferred here and the walls re-covered in cinnamon silk, which perfectly matched the existing carpet by Adam and the upholstery on Chippendale's chairs. The most important portrait is perhaps of Edwin Lascelles by Joshua Reynolds, painted in the 1760s.

the large role he played in this project, Harewood House can be considered Adam's earliest neoclassic domestic building in England. "I would not exceed the limits of expense that I always set myself," Lascelles wrote Adam. "Let us do everything properly and well, mais pas trop." The building budget for the house was a considerable thirty thousand pounds, and this was exceeded by twenty-five percent—not too bad for such a great undertaking. Most of the bills are still in the Harewood archives, many marked with Edwin Lascelle's comments.

Many of Adam's drawings for various rooms at Harewood survive in the collections of Sir John Soane's Museum in London, including forty designs for ceilings, thirty for fireplaces, and fourteen for the friezes in the main apartments. The best preserved of his rooms at Harewood are the Entrance Hall—where the visitor is distracted by a gigantic, rather over endowed 1938–40 statue by Jacob Epstein of Adam (the progenitor rather than the architect!)—the Music Room (page 81), the Cinnamon Drawing Room (page 71), the Gallery (pages 76–79), and the Old Library (pages 60, 61). Many others were altered during the Victorian period by Lady Louisa Thynne, the third Countess of Harewood, who needed to accommodate twelve children, a great many servants, Victorian comforts, and a less-formal way of living.

Robert Adam had a coterie of people who worked for him. He favored Joseph Rose and William Collins for the plasterwork, and he brought the painters Biagio Rebecca, Antonio Zucchi, and Zucchi's Austrian wife, Angelika Kauffmann, to create landscapes and mythological scenes that were an integral part of his decorative program. Although Adam designed some very beautiful furniture himself, for the most part he relied on Thomas Chippendale to design the furniture for Harewood.

Chippendale was born in 1718 at Otley in Yorkshire into a very simple family of carpenters. By the time he paid his first visit to Harewood as a potential supplier, Chippendale's beautifully illustrated book *The Gentleman and Cabinet-Maker's Directory*, was in its third edition and he was one of the most sought-after furniture makers in England. He wrote to another Yorkshire client, Sir Rowland Winn of Nostell Priory, "As soon as I got to Mr Laselles [*sic*] and look'd over the whole of the house, I found that Shou'd want a Many designs." He was absolutely correct and his total bill was close to 7,000 pounds, or twenty-five percent of what Lascelles had originally budgeted for building the palace! In addition to Chippendale's spectacular State Bedroom (pages 66, 67), Harewood is filled with seemingly endless Chippendale gilded mirrors, carved dining chairs, inlaid wine coolers, chinoiserie commodes, consoles, sets of gilded armchairs and sofas, and every other possible furnishing, all of the finest quality. Quite a lot of furniture was sold when Countess Louisa remodeled some of Adam's rooms, and perhaps some of it remains in a crate which will be found one day in a Yorkshire stable.

By 1771, the house was habitable, but there were still problems. Edwin Lascelles complained of "a water closet which stinks all over the House," a not uncommon problem at the time. By 1780, the interior had been completed. In 1795, Edwin Lascelles died childless and his cousin Edward, the first Earl of Harewood, inherited the house. The first earl put together his own orchestra, enjoyed the opera, and, when in London, had a box at Drury Lane Theater and engaged first-rate artists to perform at his various houses. In fact, he sounds rather like the present Earl! He collected Wedgwood, and was a major patron of the portraitist John Hoppner and the landscape painter J. M. W. Turner. Two large Turner landscapes dominate the Library and there is a special gallery for watercolors of Harewood House by Turner, Thomas Girtin, and John Varley, which were the result of invitations to the artists extended by the Earl and his son to stay and work at the house. In 1815, Queen Charlotte and the Prince Regent (later George IV) came to stay, and the next year Prince Nicholas Romanoff, who was to become Tsar Nicolas I in 1825, was received in State, with his entourage of sixteen, by the Earl and Countess of Harewood. Dinner, on both occasions, was served on the renowned family gold plate while fifty musicians and the local church choir performed Handel's music. Quite evidently, the enormous effort and large sums spent on building and furnishing Harewood House had been worth it and Barbados must have indeed seemed very far away.

The Harewoods customarily passed first names from father to son, and Edward Viscount Lascelles, known as "The Beau," enjoyed dressing up to the nines. He bore a remarkable resemblance to the Prince Regent, and collected Sèvres porcelain, some of which had once belonged to Marie Antoinette. The Beau, however, predeceased his father and so his younger brother Henry became the second Earl of Harewood in 1820. Henry's life consisted mostly of shooting, hunting, and attending to politics. And he was content to leave the house as it was when he inherited it. He died in 1841. This third Earl of Harewood was married to Lady Louisa Thynne, daughter of the second Marquess of Bath. She had been raised at Longleat House in Wiltshire and had seen its successful renovation and reconstruction. With a large family that would number thirteen children, the Countess immediately set about the reconstruction of Harewood House, commissioning Sir Charles Barry to do the work. He would present his plans in January 1842. Amazingly the refurbishment of the house cost more than Edwin Lascelles had spent building it. The biggest change made was the addition of the enormous Terrace on the south side of the house where previously there had been just a Palladian facade that looked over a landscape designed by Capability Brown. Brown's idea for great estates was to redesign nature by creating beautiful hills and clumps of trees where God had neglected to do so, and to never let on that man had been involved. The French and Italians followed the

The Spanish Library (preceding pages, above) was originally a dressing room that led into the State Bedroom. It was totally transformed by Barry into a library with heavy mahogany bookshelves crowned by a series of plaster busts set against a border of Córdoba leather—giving the room its new name. The leather abuts Adam's delicate frieze, cornice, and ceiling and demonstrates a Victorian insensibility to other styles. Set out on the table are royal souvenirs, including photographs of Edward VII and his sons on the Royal Yacht Britannia.

The Library (opposite) has always been a favorite gathering place for the Harewood family at Christmas. In spite of Barry's addition of mahogany bookshelves and recent modern sofas and armchairs, Adam dominates here thanks to his

sumptuous white and peach ceiling, white marble fireplaces, and the plaster over mantles by William Collins, which represent Bacchic revelers and a pagan sacrifice. On either side are important landscapes in oil by Turner, who also painted several watercolors of Harewood for Edward Lascelles.

very different path set by Le Nôtre, Louis XIV's gardener at Versailles, by taming nature through formal parterres and terraces filled with fountains and statuary. Barry's elaborate new "Italian parterre" (pages 58–59) now dominates both the house and the landscape and is the sort of extravagance that the Francophile Rothschilds added to their continental pleasure palaces in the Vale of Aylesbury.

The third earl died in 1857, and was succeeded by his son Henry who enjoyed his fortune, house, and situation until he died forty-five years later. In 1845, Henry had married Lady Elizabeth de Burgh, the daughter of the Marquess of Clanricarde, but he was a widower with motherless children when he moved into Harewood House twelve years later. The next year he married the daughter of a local landowner, Diana Elizabeth Smyth. Like many rich Victorian gentlemen, he shuttled between his houses, clubs, and the turf, and occasionally found it necessary to sell property to pay the bills his diminishing income could no longer cover. When he died in 1892, his son Henry Lascelles, the fifth earl, found himself so short of cash that his trustees severely limited any expenditures at Harewood and had to approve a special allowance of seven hundred pounds to cover the costs of a visit by King Edward VII in 1908.

Between 1905 and 1907, the fifth earl's son, Henry Lascelles, or Harry, was an honorary attaché to the British ambassador in Rome and, though his allowance was not great, he started seriously collecting paintings. Like many other aristocrats, the Harewoods had filled their house with great furniture, but thought of it as decoration. Their Cinnamon Drawing Room, Yellow Drawing Room, and Victorian Dining Room (page 80) are replete with family portraits by Sir Joshua Reynolds, Thomas Gainsborough, George Romney, Sir Thomas Lawrence, and others, but these were considered part of family history. They also had gold and silver dinner services embellished with the family arms, but these were a means of receiving their peers in the style they deserved. People's attitude toward art changed after the French Revolution when royal and aristocratic collections came on the market. When the Industrial Revolution produced vast new fortunes, art collecting became a major occupation for the new as well as the old rich. Harry's great uncle, the second Marquess of Clanricarde, was one of these new collectors. Clanricarde was a scruffy looking and quarrelsome eccentric with whom nobody wanted to converse. Harry met him by chance at his London club in 1916. He and his nephew shared an interest in art and they were, after all, related. Clanricarde took to the charming Lascelles, and was very touched that he actually wanted to talk to him. Shortly thereafter, Lord Lascelles—whose personal income was less than a thousand pounds a year—was astounded to learn that Clanricarde had left him 2,500,000 pounds, a castle in County Galway, and his collection of Italian and Flemish paintings.

The North Gallery (previous pages, opposite, and above) is one of the most magnificent rooms in Britain, thanks to its large dimensions (76 feet long by 24 feet wide), its wonderful decoration, the collection of Chinese porcelain, and the exceptional Old Master paintings hanging on the walls. The paintings were inherited by the sixth Earl of Harewood from his eccentric millionaire uncle, the Marquess of Clanricarde. The ceiling is one of Adam's finest creations. And for this room Chippendale created the two large gilded mirrors on either side of the fireplace as well as the white marble-topped gilded console tables beneath them. These tables display precious green celadon Chinese porcelain mounted in French gilt bronze. A marble statue of Cupid (opposite) by the English sculptor John Gibson stands in front of the elaborate north window, crowned by Chippendale's carved wood pelmet that simulates red damask and gold tassels. The paintings are by Titian, Tintoretto, Giovanni Bellini, Lorenzo Lotto, and Pollaiuolo, among others.

These and the Italian pictures Henry Lascelles had bought with his great uncle's legacy make up the majority of paintings hanging today in Harewood's Gallery, which include Madonnas by Giovanni Bellini, portraits by Lorenzo Lotto, Jacopo Tintoretto, and Paolo Veronese, as well as a portrait of France's King François I by Titian. There is also Pollaiuolo's *Christ at the Column* and El Greco's *Allegory*. Chippendale's gilded consoles display the magnificent collection of Chinese porcelain made during the reigns of K'ang Hsi, Yung Cheng, and Ch'ien Lung. Many of these pieces are mounted in French eighteenth-century ormolu fittings. Much of this porcelain was brought to Harewood from the family house in Hanover Square. The Gallery, an Adam creation, is beautifully lit from six tall windows framed by columns and crowned with carved and gilded pelmets from which flow short, red carved draperies. An 1827 watercolor by John Scarlett Davis shows this long gallery punctuated with stuffed armchairs and hung with family portraits. The very successful present arrangement is the brainchild of the present Earl of Harewood and the talented picture restorer Alec Cobbe.

The very last rooms to be built at Harewood were those for the Princess Royal (pages 63, 64), and they include a charming dressing room with a small salon and a ritzy marble bathroom en suite. These were designed by Sir Herbert Baker, an associate of Sir Edwin Lutyens, in the design of New Delhi. By the time the Princess died in 1965, life in England—and at Harewood—had undergone a seismic change. Two world wars, the depression, postwar shortages, and a socialist government made grand country house parties anathema, and country gentlemen had to concentrate on how to keep their stately homes rather than on how to enjoy them. The silver lining of these clouds was that they permitted a few truly talented people, such as the present earl, to develop their considerable talents and enrich the world.

All traces of Adam's decoration were removed from the State Dining Room (above), but Chippendale's twenty dining chairs have remained as have two splendid marqueterie urns and pedestals lined with lead to serve as wine coolers. Until recent times when it was sold, the sideboards and dining room table were used to present the renowned Harewood collection of gold and silver plate. The room is filled with family portraits by, among others, Thomas Lawrence, John Hoppner, and the more recent William Nicholson (1872–1949), who painted the portrait of the sixth earl over the fireplace. Roger, one of Harewood's footmen (right), is responsible for winding all the clocks at Harewood. (Opposite) The Music Room is a reflection of the first earl of Harewood who had his own orchestra and choir and was a major music patron in London. The decoration here is pure Adam, but the gilded set of tapestry-upholstered chairs was originally made for the State Dressing Room. Above the fireplace, Mary Chaloner, sister-in-law of the first earl, is represented by Joshua Reynolds as Euphrosyne in Milton's "L'Allegro."

CHÂTEAU DE HAROUÉ

La vie de château in Lorraine

Princess Minnie de Beauvau Craon was in the stately court-yard of Haroué, her massive château in eastern Lorraine, busily discussing some of the endless problems of managing such a large estate: a leak in the monogrammed slate roof that needs patching, a glitch with the plumbing, a restoration that is not advancing on schedule, a local company that has rented the place for a board meeting and wants to change the date, flower arrangements for another rental, the wedding of a couple from nearby Nancy, drugs in the village, menus for the weekend with guests from London and Paris. When I arrived, Minnie was dressed in sensible British tweeds. She had just arrived from London, where she lives most of the year, traveling nearly an entire day to visit her castle and keep it from falling apart.

Her Sri Lankan butler, Julien, sensed the arrival of a guest, and walked energetically down the long path to take my bag to a bedroom overlooking the garden. Minnie assumes the role of hostess with an ease that comes from a solid upbringing, from parents and grandparents who navigated in the highest realm of international society, and above all, from a generous spirit and a wry sense of humor. Minnie's entertaining banter, as she led me through the enormous château, never betrayed the constant preoccupations that a great house imposes on its owners. It must seem to her that generations of dukes, princes, kings, and queens who have been to visit, the people of Lorraine who take immense pride in the finest ancestral home of the region, and her predecessors who spent most of their lives at Haroué, are all saying, "Don't let us down, keep up the standard, don't sell the furniture, do you really need the rent of those people who want to bask in our glory? Do you have to be so courteous to those local bureaucrats whose ancestors cut off our ancestors' heads?" Everybody knows that castles might have ghosts, and when you may have to spend a few nights alone in one, it is important to keep everybody, including the departed, happy and out of sight.

The large, light, antique-filled bedroom, where a breakfast of steaming coffee and warm croissants will arrive the next morning on a silver tray with the Paris newspapers, has a broad, plump bed with an elegantly faded spread and mono-grammed, slightly shiny pillows. A rested, relaxed guest will reciprocate good hospitality with entertaining and interesting talk, and keep up the standard of the distinguished predecessors who have slept in his room over the last two hundred years. High standards of conversation are one of the staples of château life in France, and those who cannot keep up are not asked back. You must have at your fingertips the latest political and social gossip, must have read the most interesting new

(Previous pages) The Château de Haroué seen from a garden designed by Russell Page in the 1930s. Although the house was built in the eighteenth century, the turrets are a throwback to the Middle Ages, as if to indicate that Marc de Beauveau Craon, the builder, had been around Lorraine for a long time, which was not the case. The main façade (opposite) is true to its period. It is a masterpiece by Germain Boffrand, one of Louis XIV's architects, who was brought to Nancy in 1700 to design a new palace for the Duke of Lorraine. Lunéville was, in fact, a clone of Versailles on a smaller scale. Nine years later, he became First Architect of the Duke and worked on the Place Stanislas in Nancy, one of the most beautiful squares in France. From there, Marc de Beauveau brought a series of statues by Guibal that were placed on a bridge over the moat leading to the courtyard (above).

books, seen the best exhibitions, have strong and original opinions, and been to the most controversial opera productions in Aix, Salzburg, or at the Bastille. A friendly, American-style, "What are you busy with now?" simply won't do, and arrival in a brilliant salon, such as that of Haroué, can cause the sort of butterflies in your tummy that you last remembered when taking a college exam.

The job of a châtelaine is to instantly remove these butterflies, make a guest feel at home, put everybody at ease, as Minnie does now with an invitation to tea in the library, a few steps down a corridor (opposite) filled with muddy boots, children's bicycles, tennis rackets, coat hooks festooned with raincoats, tweed caps, wool scarves, and whatever else is needed for long and chatty walks in the countryside. When asked the secret of a successful visit, Minnie will say it is good food and wine, which she provides with wonderful dishes prepared by her cook Evelyne, who has been in the house for many years, and with the ministrations of Lucien, who butlered for many years in the houses and on the yacht of the late Greek ship owners Basil and Elise Goulandris. Minnie could also add to her short list of secrets flowers and dinner-table decoration by her good friend Bruno Roy, who organizes many of the top balls and weddings in Paris, and who arrives at Haroué in a car filled with fresh flowers he picks up at the Rungis market outside Paris. Having a butler, cook, and part-time maid may seem like a luxury until you count up the rooms and the guests, and then you wonder how she does it.

The corridor that connects the downstairs bedrooms with Minnie's cozy, everyday living room leads to a monumental, sweeping staircase (above right) designed by the house's architect, Germain Boffrand. Its forged iron railing with crossed Cs of the Craon family was made in 1735 by Jean Lamour. Lamour, along with Jules Hardouin Mansart, (First Architect of France's King Louis XIV), the Italian stage designer Ferdinando Bibiena, Boffrand, and others of equal talent created the celebrated Place Stanislas in nearby Nancy. Named after Stanislas Leczcynski, once king of Poland, the square was mostly built by his father Léopold. One could argue that the square is as beautiful and impressive as the Place de la Concorde or the Place Vendôme in Paris.

We have tea in the library (pages 90–91), a room that has the sobriety of the finest Régence rooms, with its sumptuous paneling and carved Corinthian columns. It was also designed by Boffrand, and it has an entire wall of shelves lined with eighteenth-century bound-leather books, many relating to the Beauvau Craon family. Above the marble fireplace is a portrait of Louis XV in a marble *trumeau*, also designed by Boffrand. Family portraits fill the walls, and round tables skirted in sumptuous velvet are covered with bibelots and family related photographs, including those of a ten-day visit the late Queen Elizabeth, the Queen Mother, paid to Haroué (page 98). The visit was a great success, according to Minnie. Courtiers filled

Haroué today is very much a living house, as cherished by its present owner, Princess Minnie de Beauveau, as it was by her father, Marc, seen together (below) in 1959. A corridor to the guest rooms (opposite) leads to a grand staircase (above), whose eighteenth-century railing contains the crossed Cs of Craon. Off the corridors are a series of sunlit, antique-filled, charming guest rooms filled with chintz-upholstered sofas, good books in French and English, soft pillows, wooden shutters, and heavy curtains to shut out the light. The comfortable bathrooms date back to the 1920s, and Minnie's guests like to gather in her living room at the end of the corridor (opposite). The traditional French *vie de château* enjoyed here includes country walks, bicycling, good food and wine, and, above all, sophisticated conversation.

A corridor overlooking the courtyard leads to another series of bedrooms (above), where guests are served hot coffee and croissants for breakfast, accompanied by the morning newspapers from Paris and Nancy (left). In more formal times, the guests were served by footmen in livery. All that remains of them today are buttons from their livery (opposite). The library (overleaf) is the center of the château's social life in the cooler months of the year. This wonderful eighteenth-century room is filled with family mementos and portraits. Over the fireplace and in the *trumeau*, designed by Boffrand, is a portrait of Louis XV. The Beauveau Craons were leading art collectors in France, but most of their treasures have been sold to keep up the house.

all the rooms for the first time since the French Revolution, and Haroué relived its glory days once again. Here are photographs of Minnie's children, Victoria and Sebastian, who live in England and come back every summer with their own children. They take long bicycle rides in the hilly Lorraine terrain, lounge around a swimming pool, enjoy picnics and barbecues, and become imbued with the glorious heritage of their family. There are also pictures of Minnie's handsome father, Prince Marc de Beauvau Craon (page 87), her mother, Cristina, and her uncle Antenor Patiño, the son of a Bolivian magnate Don Simon Patiño, known as "the tin king," thanks to his one-time monopoly of this essential metal.

The library is the social center of château life, and, despite the grandeur and formality of the family portraits that line its walls, it radiates great warmth thanks to a large and thick Oriental carpet, comfortable upholstered silk and velvet sofas and armchairs, sun that shines through the high French doors, and flaming logs in Boffrand's carved fireplace. A door at one end of the library leads to a formal paneled dining room (page 94) with eight mahogany armchairs and forty straight chairs (all of royal provenance), a splendid seventeenth-century tapestry representing a battle between Alexander the Great and the Persian King Darius, and four large panels of the seasons

The first Prince Marc de Beauveau Craon (left), can be considered the founder of his princely line. His titles, coat of arms (above), and fortune were derived from a close friendship with Duke Léopold of Lorraine, his childhood friend, as recompense for his great talents as a diplomat. He was made a prince by Louis XV and his Treaty of Ryswick led, in the long run, to Lorraine's reversion to France. He negotiated the marriage of François Étienne de Lorraine to Maria Theresa of Austria, and he married Anne-Marguerite de Ligneville, the Duchess of Lorraine's Lady in Waiting, whose chambre d'apparat is on the ground floor of Haroué (opposite). It contains her husband's portrait and tapestries relating to the life of Alexander the Great that were a wedding present from Duke Léopold.

of the year painted by Baron Gérard. The dining room in turn leads to the absolutely enchanting, small, round Salon Pillement (page 94) located in one of the four towers of the château. Jean Baptiste Pillement, a renowned French landscape painter who also worked in Portugal, executed the Chinoiserie frescoes of this room around 1750, and the salon was used at that time by Princess Anne Marguerite de Beauvau Craon for her musical soirées. Today, Minnie uses the rooms for small lunches and candlelit dinners, constantly varying the flower arrangements, glassware, and porcelain.

From the library, dining room, and Salon Pillement, one looks out onto a formal French garden created not by Louis XIV's gardener, François Lenôtre, as might seem appropriate for a grand château of this period, but by Emilio Terry in 1952 (page 105). A good friend of Minnie's father, Terry was a highly appreciated, talented, and very social decorator in Paris, who designed anything his friends wanted from costume balls to garden pavilions. The garden is cut off from the house by a moat and linked to the house by a grand staircase embellished with statues of grouped putti by Barthélemy Guibal which were once on the Place Stanislas, as were those in the courtyard entrance (page 84). The garden's elements are simple and formal to the extreme— tall boxwood hedges, geometric topiaries, rectangular-shaped parterres framed by gravel paths, and a group of eighteenth-century statues, all of which blend in beautifully with the low hills and forests of Lorraine just beyond.

A door at the other end of the library leads to an enfilade of stately, paneled, mostly unfurnished rooms, except for a vitrine of ceremonial family silver and an occasional tapestry or mirror. Such are the exigencies of keeping up the house that Minnie often rents out these rooms and keeps them empty for convenience's sake. Nearly all of the house's magnificent eighteenth-century furniture has been sold, replaced, or removed to Paris. Revolution, wars, gambling debts, and life at court have taken their toll on the family fortune over time, and going through auction catalogues gives us an idea of the importance of the de Beauvau Craon collections. On Friday, April 21, 1865, for example, the following pieces were sold by the family at the Hotel Drouot in Paris: a precious *petit bureau de dame* of the Louis XVI period embellished with Japanese lacquer panels and bronze gilt caryatid feet by Gouthière and offered by Queen Marie Antoinette to Madame de Senone, one of her ladies in waiting; a very fine marquetry commode with gilt bronze decoration, including the initials of Queen Marie Antoinette by Gouthière; a marquetry console with bronze gilt ornamentation by J. H. Riesner; an ebony coffer with Florentine inlaid marble representing birds and foliage in lapis and jasper; a Boulle clock; a very large Louis XIII bureau with tin inlay; a cup in red Sicilian jasper with gilt bronze mounts by Gouthière; Gouthière candelabras, torches, and inkwell; two Canalettos depicting the Piazza San Marco and the Rialto Bridge; a portrait of Louise de Lorraine by François Clouet; a

portrait of Marie Anne Schotten by Van Dyck; and much, much more.

Haroué's name derives from the word *gué*, a ford, which is nearby on the Madon River. The first family to move on to the property took the name. When their clan died out, the property passed to the Bassompierres by marriage. The extant fortress was transformed into a Renaissance castle and in 1579, François de Bassompierre, the most remarkable member of the family, was born here. A handsome and courageous Renaissance warrior, François became a Maréchal of France in 1622, negotiated the Treaty of Madrid in 1621, was a prolific author and member of the Académie française, and was a renowned Lothario. One of his flirtations inspired Hugo von Hoffmannstahl's libretto for the Richard Strauss opera *Die Frau Ohne Schatten*. However, Bassompierre's overriding ambition involved him in a plot against the French king Henri II, as a result of which he was imprisoned at the Bastille for twelve years, his lands were confiscated, and his castle ravaged. When he died in 1646, all that was left of Haroué was the moat and what is now called the Bassompierre Courtyard, which is used as stables. Nothing much occurred at Haroué until Duke Léopold of Lorraine made his childhood friend, Marc de Beauvau Craon (opposite below), Constable of Lorraine in

1719, and handed over the property to him in perpetuity. Lorraine was originally part of Lotharingia, a kingdom assigned in 843 to Emperor Lothair I during the first division of the Carolingian empire, which originally covered what is today the Netherlands, Belgium, Luxembourg, Lorraine, Alsace, and northwestern Germany. Lothair also received Italy and Burgundy. In 959, the empire was divided into the duchies of Lower Lorraine in the north and Upper Lorraine in the South, and each had an appointed Duke as leader. In Upper Lorraine, where Haroué is located, the ducal title continued until 1766 with a grand and elaborate court in Nancy throughout the year, and in Lunéville during the summers. Lorraine is the land of Joan of Arc and Charles de Gaulle, a place of fanatic patriotism that has a history of disagreements with France over control of the territory, and was often occupied by French soldiers. Lorraine and neighboring Alsace later became a point of contention between France and Germany, stemming from the Franco-Prussian War of 1870–71, which had led to the first German occupation of Paris and the downfall of the Emperor Napoleon III. The region reverted to France after World War I, was annexed by Germany during World War II (1940–1944), and reverted back again to France with the defeat of the Nazis.

Thanks to the intervention of Duke Léopold, Marc de Beauveau Craon was made Viceroy of Tuscany and a Spanish grandee, and he was elevated to the rank of Prince by Louis XV. In 1704 he married Anne Marguerite de Ligniville, scion of one of Lorraine's top four families, and future lady-in-waiting to the Duchess of Lorraine. The sister of Louis XIV and mother-in-law of Duke Léopold, the Princess of the Palatinate wrote of Ann Marguerite, "She has the finest figure in the world, and a lovely, delicately colored, practically white skin. Her most enchanting feature is her mouth, her teeth are admirable, and she laughs charmingly." Léopold must have agreed, because he fell in love with her, and as of 1709, this liaison became quite official. He showered her with presents while she reigned over the court at Lunéville, and he left her a good part of his fortune. At Haroué, following through the emptied *defilé* of salons on the ground floor, one may still see Princess Anne-Marguerite's sumptuous, Versailles-like reception bedroom (page 93) and its red silk *lit d'apparat*, embroidered in gold thread with the de Beauvau Craon-Ligniville coats of arms. On the walls hang Flemish tapestries with scenes from the life of Alexander the Great, which were a wedding present from Duke Léopold to Marc and his bride.

Marc de Beauvau seems to have taken his wife's infidelities in stride, as was usual in prearranged marriages. Undoubtedly becoming closer to Léopold had its advantages, particularly when the duke covered the huge gambling debts the prince incurred, mainly in horse racing and at the billiard table. Prince Marc also spent lavishly on his library and collected more than four hundred pictures, including works by Rembrandt, Poussin, and Claude Lorrain. He undertook the building of a new château at Haroué on the site of the old one, an enterprise that was to last from 1720 to 1729. It is not surprising that the prince chose Germain Boffrand as his architect, since Boffrand had designed the family's *hôtel particulier* in Nancy, and was responsible for the palace that Duke Léopold built at Lunéville.

The Salon Pillement (opposite and overleaf), painted in 1750, is located in one of the castle's turrets, and is the only Chinoiserie room in Lorraine. Similar examples can be found in Chantilly, at the Château de Champs, and at the Hôtel de Rohan in Paris. It is used as a small dining room, and these days Minnie de Beauveau invents a new *décor de table* for each meal. It is adjacent to a larger room (above right) used for formal dinner parties and which has equally imaginative table decorations. In this room is another of the Alexander the Great tapestries, and part of the Louis

XVIII furniture ordered by the king for his Château de Saint Ouen and left in his will to his friend the Comtesse d'Ayla, a Beauveau Craon by marriage. Julien, the butler lights the candles just before dinner is served.

(Above) In the library, a framed photograph of the late Queen Elizabeth, the Queen Mother, recalls her visit to the château.
(Opposite) A bottle of champagne is set out for guests on an Empire gueridon in the Salon de Musique on the first floor of the château. The wonderful gilded Louis XVIII furniture was ordered by the king from the ébéniste Bellangé for his Saint-Ouen château, and Louis XVIII also commissioned his own portrait from Baron Gérard (overleaf left) and the portrait of his beloved Comtesse Zoé de Cayla (overleaf, above right). The king, whose effigy is on the terracotta bust on the Empire gueridon next to the floral bouquet, was very much in love with the countess and protected her from an irascible husband. When she died, Zoé left 1,500 letters from the king. They had often written to each other several times a day.
Charles Louis de Beauveau, the grand nephew of the countess, inherited Haroué and his Italian wife, Minnie Gregorini, brought to the house her collection of letters from Verdi and Puccini.

Boffrand was born in Nantes, the son of an architect, and was introduced to the court of the Sun King by his uncle, Philippe Quinault, who was one of the king's *valets de chambre* and wrote the very popular *Armida* that was set to music by both Gluck and Lully. Boffrand studied sculpture with François Girardon and architecture with Jules Mansart, and was a creditable engineer, metallurgist, physicist, stonecutter, and arch builder. He was part of Mansart's inner circle, but between Mansart's death in 1708 and the Sun King's demise in 1715, official architecture waned in France because all available funds had been spent on Versailles. Boffrand became an entrepreneur, building *hôtels particuliers* on speculation, and accepted other commissions abroad. He gained his reputation thanks to town houses he designed and built for the nephew of Charles Le Brun, First Painter of the King, and then for Anne Palatine of Bavaria, Duchess of Maine and a mistress of the French Regent, the Duc d'Orléans.

In post-Louis XIV days, the grave Baroque of Bernini gave way to the frivolous Rococo style that came from Germany and Austria, seen in the licentious paintings of Boucher and Fragonard. Boffrand resisted this tendency thanks to his latent Jansenism and inherent classicism. In 1700, Mansart was invited to Nancy, where he started work on plans for a new ducal palace. The Duc d'Orléans had presented Boffrand to the Duke of Lorraine, and Boffrand started working for him in 1702, when Léopold was in the planning stage of his large summer palace in Lunéville. Voltaire aptly writes that, "You could not believe that you had changed palaces when moving from Versailles to Lunéville." Indeed, Lunéville seems to be a clone of the Sun King's palace, albeit on a smaller scale. Versailles set the tone for all royal palaces to come, but only Duke Léopold and the Mad King Ludwig of Bavaria took the plans so literally! Boffrand became First Architect to the Duke of Lorraine in 1709, the same year that he became an academician and started work on the Palais du Petit Luxembourg on the Rue de Vaugirard in Paris, an annex to the larger palace built for Maria de Medici.

From the Court of Lorraine to Haroué was an obvious step. At Haroué, Boffrand created for the prince a castle with a medieval look thanks to its towers on the four angles, each coiffed by watch turrets, and the moat that he left in place. This was a throwback to a building style popular in the fifteenth and sixteenth centuries and perhaps Marc de Beauveau wanted to send a message to those approaching his castle that he had been around the Lorraine for longer than was really the case. *Aprés tout*, he was from Anjou and had received his princely title from a French king. Boffrand's classical colonnade and sculpted pediment with the family arms at the entrance of the house (page 87) would be at home in any of the aristocratic districts of Paris. It is rather a jolt to a visitor who has just passed the small, rather ugly modern buildings of the local village, not to speak of its purple and yellow street lamps. Also true to the

eighteenth century is the château's interior decoration, much of which is owed to Boffrand himself. The château was sumptuously furnished, and great festivities were planned when the house was finally finished in 1729. But Duke Léopold had an accident and died that spring, and so instead of celebrating the completion of his château Marc de Beauvau followed Léopold's coffin in the funerary procession, carrying the great Constable's sword, which is now on display in a vitrine at Haroué.

The Prince and Princess de Beauvau had twenty children, of which thirteen survived. The oldest son, Charles Juste, was to become a member of the Académie française, a minister of Louis XVI, and the next châtelain when his father died in 1754. His sister Marie Catherine married the Marquis de Bouffleurs, and she was considered one of the wittiest ladies at the French court, a brilliant *salonière*, and a sort of second queen of Lunéville, when Stanislas Leczynski succeeded his father Léopold as Duke of Lorraine. Stanislas was a very popular ruler, and when his daughter Marie Antoinette became Queen of France, the duke enjoyed his increased influence at Versailles. Stanislas often stayed at Haroué before his death in 1766. Shortly thereafter, notwithstanding Marie Antoinette, Louis XVI severely limited the independence of Lorraine and closed down the courts at Lunéville and Nancy. Now Charles Juste

Views of the upstairs rooms with more furniture left by King Louis XVIII to Zoé. Her daughter Valentine married the younger brother of Prince Marc de Beauveau, then head of the family, who had auctioned off much of the magnificent family furniture, and sold the château itself to a brewer in 1865, the year after his father Charles died. Zoé saved the family honor by buying back Haroué and, not having a male heir, left the château and everything she had inherited from the king to her grand nephew Charles-Louis, who was only six years old at the time. In 1920, he married an Italian heiress, Minnie Gregorini Bingham, seen together (right). Minnie decided to move into Haroué and restore what was in ruinous condition. (Overleaf) Details of the Imperial Room, inspired by the Cabinet des Muses at the Hôtel Lambert in Paris, which was created by Prince Charles Juste de Beauveau to receive the Emperor Napoleon III.

played an important rule in France's history, becoming governor of Languedoc and Marseilles, and later accompanying the royal family on their humiliating trip from Versailles to the Bastille after the French Revolution broke out in 1789. He had no male heir and left Haroué to his nephew Marc Étienne de Beauvau Craon, who became châtelain in 1790, was appointed Chamberlain at the court of Napoleon I in 1810, and enrolled his two sons in the Imperial French army. His son Charles, who eventually inherited Haroué, was left for dead in a Russian battlefield during the dreadful Russian campaign of 1812 but survived to marry twice. His second wife, the young Polish Ludmilla Komar, studied with the painter Hébert, while her sister Delphine, the Countess Potocka, was the pupil of Frédéric Chopin. Chopin often stayed at Haroué, gave concerts there, and dedicated several compositions to the Komar sisters.

Charles and Ludmilla decided to invite France's new Emperor Napoleon III to Haroué and created an imperial bedroom on the first floor to mark the occasion (pages 102, 103), commissioning Hébert to design and execute (with the aid of Ludmilla and her sisters) the decoration of the room. It was to be a copy of the *Cabinet des Muses* by Eustache Lesueur at the renowned Hôtel Lambert in Paris, which belonged to their Polish friends the Czartoryskis. Hébert first came in 1859, and the room was nearly finished in 1860. Just before the arrival of the emperor, Charles got up on a ladder to put on some finishing touches, fell, and never recovered. The imperial visit was canceled. Charles died a cripple in 1864, and in 1865 came the previously mentioned sale of many of Haroué's finest treasures. That very year, the new heir, Prince Marc de Beauvau, sold Haroué to a local brewer. The following day his sister-in-law Valentine de Beauvau (née Du Cayla) bought back the house intending to leave it to her son, thus keeping Haroué in the family. However, he died shortly afterwards.

Valentine's mother, Zöé Victoire, had a remarkable life. She had been married to Count Achille Du Cayala, with whom she had two children, Valentine and a son, Ugolin. A beautiful lady, Zöé had an irascible husband and a few very prominent lovers to make her life more agreeable. Her mother-in-law, before dying, wrote a letter to France's King Louis XVIII, asking him to protect Zöé from the fury of her husband. In 1817, Zöé visited the monarch in person to ask him to prevent the count from taking away her children. The king was instantly taken with the thirty-two-year-old countess. He asked her back, and thereafter, they scheduled meetings every Wednesday and wrote each other several times a week. She became his mistress and the subject of much gossip and

speculation. The king gave Zöé many gifts, including the ruined Château Saint-Ouen, which he magnificently rebuilt and refurnished for her. For the château, he commissioned Baron Gérard to paint a large canvas of the king in his study, four panels of the seasons, and a portrait of the lovely Zöé with her children. He also ordered from the *maître ébéniste* Bellangé a vast quantity of furniture, all of which is at Haroué today (page 99–101). The château's opening festivities came on May 2, 1823, and the highlight was a lunch in the orangerie for eight hundred people with decorations by the painter Isabey. The next year, the king died leaving Saint-Ouen and its contents to Zöé.

Zöé's grand nephew, Charles-Louis de Beauvau, became Valentine's heir at the tender age of six, inheriting Haroué, which his mother had bought, and Saint-Ouen which had come from her mother. There were a great many lawsuits about the ownership of Haroué, and the château remained empty for many years while Charles-Louis lived at his own estate at Sainte-Assise near Paris. In 1920, he married an Italian heiress, Minnie Gregorini Bingham. She was a close friend of Verdi and Puccini, and they wrote her wonderful letters that are preserved today at Haroué. The Italian Minnie fell instantly in love with the castle in Lorraine. Charles-Louis sold Sainte-Assise, restored Haroué, which had fallen into dis-

repair, moved in Louis XVIII's furniture and paintings, and the château entered a brilliant period. Charles-Louis and Minnie were much appreciated fixtures of international society. They attended the famous costume balls of the 1930s, were photographed by Horst and Hoyningen-Huene, and appeared in all the fashion magazines. Minnie wrote in a letter to her friend Maurice Barrès that it was in Lorraine that her new life took off and found its true purpose.

In 1942, their son Marc became châtelain at a time when he was fully occupied with the Free French movement of Charles de Gaulle in London and the Resistance in Lorraine. He worked hard on the house's preservation, opened it to the public in 1964, and became very involved in the politics of the region. He died suddenly in 1982 and his daughter Minnie became the new châtelaine. Though deeply cognizant of the role played by her father and his second wife, Laure, in the history of Haroué, Minnie attributes the rebirth of the house to her grandmother, whose husband sold about 5 000 acres of land near Paris in order to put a new roof on Haroué and repair its facade. This alone gives an idea of the family's courage and the legacy that Minnie upholds every day.

PALAZZO GANGI

The Palace
of a Leopard in Palermo
by Gioacchino Lanza Tomasi

Sicily became a sort of backwater in the twentieth century, a poverty stricken island between Europe and Africa filled with, mafiosi and crime. Earthquakes, volcanoes, and pickpockets, not to speak of hot winds, discouraged visitors despite the magnificence of Sicily's landscapes and seaside resorts, the ancient ruins of Segesta and Selinute, the Norman treasures, palaces, and churches in Palermo, and the large country estates at Bagheria. What had also seriously declined was the life style of a once immensely rich aristocracy who had lived a life of leisure, great ease, luxury, and sophistication. All this was brought back to life by *The Leopard*, a novel by Giuseppe Tomasi di Lampedusa, much of which took place in houses like the Palazzo Gangi, which had been occupied by Lampedusa's relatives and friends. In this and other such palaces there were magnificent balls and costume parties, highly cultivated conversation with Europe's great writers, composers, and aristocrats who were regular visitors.

The Palazzo Gangi, which stands in the Piazza Croce dei Vespri in Palermo, is rightly considered to be the most important and spectacular example of eighteenth-century Sicilian architecture. It was built within the perimeter of the city walls, which date from the reign of Frederick II. The walled city took its final form in the fifteenth century, and that is documented in views of the city that date back as early as the late sixteenth century. Palermo shrank in population following the War of the Sicilian Vespers. By the middle of the fourteenth century, the city's population is estimated to have been just above 12,000, a result of the ravages of the Black Death, the notorious Europe-wide outbreak of the bubonic plague that was especially lethal in Sicily. Population growth in the historic central city, swelling the number of inhabitants from 25,000 to 250,000, slowly transformed the cityscape.

In the fifteenth century all the important buildings in the walled city had extensive gardens. Some buildings within a garden belonging to the Commenda della Magione (the endowment of the Norman Church of the Magione granted by Frederick II to the Teutonic Order, whose Grand Master Friedrich von Salza was also chancellor of the Holy Roman Empire). These were deeded in 1475 to the nobleman Giovanni Reggio who started to build a town palace on this land. This is the first nucleus of what would become the Palazzo Gangi. In those days Palermo still belonged to the cultural sphere of the southern Mediterranean, an area that included Catalonia, Provence, Naples, and Palermo, and was still faithful to late

(Preceding pages) Tiled floor of the gallery representing *The Labors of Hercules*, designed by Andrea Gigante. Neapolitan manufactory, third quarter of the eighteenth century. Entrance to staircase (above) by Andrea Gigante, third quarter of the eighteenth century. Main entrance on Piazza Croce dei Vespri (right). Nearly all Palermo's historical buildings underwent extensive transformations over the centuries. The first archival mention of the Gangi palace dates to the late fifteenth century. The door's design is related to the adjacent courtyard with its columns in the Tuscan order. The façade on the Piazza reveals changes in taste and function. The two vases on top of the columns, probably added a hundred years later, have a gracious baroque elegance. The whole façade seems somehow frozen in time by the restorations directed by Ernesto Basile, the greatest Art Nouveau Italian architect.

(Opposite) Entrance hall with a bust of Giuseppe Mantegna, late nineteenth century. The chandeliers and the elaborate, operatic chest are part of the Victorian refurnishing of the palace.

gothic, especially Catalan, style. It was within this cultural context that the building was first erected, as can be observed in other surviving palaces of the early sixteenth century such as Abbatellis, Aiutamicristo, Marchese, and Termini Alliata. In 1578 the palazzo was sold to Giovanni Barresi e Santapau. The Santapaus were a powerful family of Catalonian descent. Giovanni's daughter Elisabetta married the Prince of Trabia, and their son Ottavio Lanza inherited the palace. The earliest surviving section of the palazzo, the *quadriporticus* courtyard in the Tuscan order, dates from this period. The Quattro Canti (literally, "four corners") of Palermo, also known as the "Teatro del Sole," designed by Mariano Smeriglio and Giulio Lasso, dates from roughly the same years. This period marked the full flourishing of Mannerist architecture, which adhered to Sebastiano Serlio's *Regole Generali di Architettura*, the foundation for the classical style that would dominate Palermo until well into the eighteenth century, and eliminate the surviving traces of the preceding Provençal-Catalonian style. The palace is mentioned in 1615 by Cavaliere Di Giovanni, who describes it as the "sumptuous beginnings of a palazzo, completed only from the foundations to the first order."

In 1652 Ottavia Lanza sold the palace to Girolamo Gravina, Prince of Gravina. Girolamo's daughter and sole heir,

The furnishings of the Gangi palace reveal a princely residence at the center of social life in Palermo's Belle Époque. At the turn of the previous century, royalty and grandees frequently visited Palermo. Political plots of imperialistic expansion in Africa were behind the recurrent visits of Kaiser Wilhelm II and King Edward VII. Signed photographs of these and other royals are on display in Palermo's palaces, but Palazzo Gangi exhibits the richest and best preserved such collection. Cavaliere Mantegna and his son, the first Mantegna prince, also hosted Richard Wagner and his huge family at the time the composer was working on the opera *Parsifal*. On the Louis XVI chest of drawers (above), amid Neapolitan and English faience, there is the portrait of Giovanna Alliata Valguarnera. She married Cavalier Giuseppe Mantegna in 1842, bringing palace and title into the Mantegna family.

The dining room of the palazzo (this page and opposite) is a jewel of Sicilian Louis XVI style. The oval shape, the bright, pleasant pilasters, the delicate gilding of the original paneling and consoles, the beautiful tiled floor with the Valguarnera coat of arms, probably commissioned in Naples, the charming fresco at the center of the vault, one of the best works of Giuseppe Velasco, known in Palermo as the Sicilian Velázquez, make this the most enjoyable space for princely private life. Prince Giuseppe Emanuele commissioned the classicist architect Giovanni Battista Cascione to design the dining room at the end of the eighteenth century. Apart from the consoles, the furniture is late nineteenth century. The elegant modulation of light reveals the

hand of an architect exerting his skills in a charming Louis XVI revival style. Perhaps this was Ernesto Basile, who was in charge of the renovations from 1906 to 1927. Princess Gangi cherishes this space and is seen (below) arranging the flowers.

Marianna, married Giuseppe Valguarnera, Prince of Valguarnera, in 1685. He died in 1699, however, and when the widowed Marianna Gravina married her second husband Giuseppe Bosco e Sandoval, Prince of Cattolica, part of her dowry was the palace. Giuseppe Bosco died in 1733 and, upon his death, the palace once again become the property of the Valguarneras.

Prince Francesco Saverio Valguarnera, Giuseppe's eldest son, had only one child, a deaf-mute daughter named Marianna after her mother. To keep the Valguarnera estates and the Gravina dowry from being lost, Marianna married her uncle Pietro Valguarnera, Giuseppe's brother, in 1749 when she was eighteen years old. According to the Sicilian laws of inheritance, an unmarried daughter had priority over male cousins. This rule followed the procedure adopted for the transfer of the kingdom of Sicily to the Swabian dynasty, whose emperor Henry VI had become king of Sicily when he arranged for Constance, the unmarried daughter of King Roger II of Hauteville, to leave her convent so that he could marry her. The Latin terminology that described the legal status of such female heirs was *virgo in capillis*, or virgin before tonsure. Marianna Valguarnera was a noteworthy person about whom the Italian author Dacia Maraini, a present-day descendant, wrote a biographical novel in 1990.

Marianna's uncle and husband, Pietro Valguarnera, was one of the master builders of the Sicilian nobility. In the common parlance of Palermo, these aristocrats were afflicted with the "mal della pietra," or "stone sickness," meaning that they built with reckless disregard for cost, and often drove themselves to financial ruin. Clear evidence of this is seen in the many unfinished palaces and villas in Palermo, whose builders had squandered their fortunes. Pietro Valguarnera was responsible for the reconstruction of the Villa Valguarnera in Bagheria, which had been begun by his mother Marianna and continued by his father Giuseppe, as well as the eighteenth-century renovation of the Palazzo Gangi. The palace that Marianna Gravina brought to Giuseppe as part of her dowry was badly run down. The prince incurred significant debt in rebuilding it.

Giuseppe Lazzara drew up a plan of the city of Palermo dated 1703, and the palace is shown in this plan as three separate sections. Only the section built around a courtyard can be said to belong to the courtly building style. The palace became part of the Valguarnera and Gravina estate in 1749. Prince Pietro commissioned the architect Andrea Gigante to enlarge and renovate the palace in the Louis XV style. Gigante was a Trapani-born clergyman, as was his teacher, Giovanni Biagio Amico, the author of the most important treatise on the Sicilian Rococo, *L'architetto pratico*, published in Palermo in 1750. This style incorporated all the theatrical innovations of the grand architecture of the seventeenth and eighteenth centuries, from Guarini and Juvarra to Ferdinando Galli Bibiena. The earliest studies of Palazzo Gangi, in fact, identified the architect as the Messina-born Filippo Juvarra, builder to the

house of Savoy and to the Spanish branch of the Bourbons. This was totally unfounded. All of the architects working in Palermo during the seventeenth and eighteenth centuries were members of religious orders, and many of them had studied within their own orders in Rome. The entire succession of official Architects of the Senate (a title that meant they were architects to the city council of Palermo), from Mariano Smeriglio and Paolo Amato to Nicolò Palma and Andrea Gigante, were clergymen. On the other hand, higher education in Palermo was reserved solely for Theatines and Jesuits. Aside from their studies in Rome, these architects studied both treatises and engravings extensively. As a result, Baroque Palermo appears to have been notably up-to-date on the Roman tradition and French models. The Architects of the Senate supplied all sorts of plans and designs over the course of two centuries, from actual buildings to decorations for events and celebrations, stage sets, and even designs for furniture and silver objects.

Gigante was the most fashionable architect during the third quarter of the eighteenth century. In Palazzo Gangi he was responsible for the major rocaille ornamentation found in the Gallery of Mirrors and in the monumental staircase. He also designed and built the most renowned Rococo monumental

The dining room still preserves the scents and flavors of formal life in the old days. A collection of nineteenth century menus (above left) can be found in one of the drawers of the consoles. They date back to the time of Princess Giulia, grandmother of the current Prince Giuseppe. Formal dinners and, especially, balls required a substantial supply of silverware. The beautiful tureen and sterling serving dishes (opposite) bear the Mantegna coat of arms. They are typical of the resilience of rocaille design beyond the second half of the nineteenth century. The silver cutlery (above right) bears more clearly the Mantegna di Gangi coat of arms. The finely chiseled silver cutlery with a late Louis-Philippe design is displayed on a tablecloth with the embroidered arms of the Alliata family. The double eagle under the princely crown alludes to the title of Princes of the Holy Roman Empire, bestowed on the family by the Austrian Habsburg emperor to which all the Alliata males are entitled. All this in today's Sicily belongs to the past, but the souls of the owners and

builders are still present with their struggle for pride and social eminence. (Above) A member of the palace staff polishing the silver. The ballroom (overleaf), set for cocktails. This room displays the portrait of Marianna Valguarnera. She was married to her uncle Pietro who commissioned the renovation of the palace by the architect Andrea Gigante.

The three antechambers to the ballroom were refurbished in Louis XVI style by Prince Pietro Emanuele at the end of the eighteenth century. At the turn of the century Palermo's aristocracy was caught by a passion for chinaware. Every palace presented large showcases holding collections of porcelain and bisque. The furnishing of these three drawing rooms was renovated by Prince Benedetto, Cavalliere Mantegna's son. The first antechamber (above) displays the porcelain collection.
(Left) A collection of fans. The third antechamber (opposite) leads to the ballroom. (Overleaf) The middle salon, the Salon of the Grotesques. Its vaulted ceiling was decorated in 1749 with frescoes in the Pompeian style. The full-length portrait depicts Princess Giulia, née Alliata di Montereale, a famous beauty and grandmother of the present owner, Prince Giuseppe. Late nineteenth-century French coffee cups and Sicilian pastries (cassatine) on a Neapolitan "Del Vecchio" faience dish adorn a table.

staircase in Palermo in the Palazzo Bonagia in the Via Alloro, less than five hundred meters from Palazzo Gangi. These projects belong to the first period of Gigante's work in Palermo, in the Palazzo Bonagia in the Via Alloro, less than five hundred meters from Palazzo Gangi. These projects belong to the first period of Gigante's work in Palermo, when he was between twenty and thirty years old. After 1770, Gigante adopted the Louis XVI style, and designed the façades of Palazzo Mazzarino on the Via Maqueda and of Villa Lanza Camastra; the latter had an Italian-style garden, and Gigante made the design for its majolica floor. He is also identified as the architect of Villa Inguaggiato in Bagheria, which is clad in carved tufa stone and adorned with festoons and other ornaments that are clearly of French influence.

We find Andrea Gigante on the Valguarnera payroll as early as 1756, and the following year he signed a contract for the construction at the palace of a new *cavallerizza* (a building for stables and carriages) with a ballroom to be built above it. Mention is also made of the new Gallery of Mirrors, whose structural work was completed in 1758. The gallery is the best-known room in the Palazzo Gangi, its unique feature being a punctured, vaulted ceiling which gives the impression of a double-layered vault. In reality the main vault supports fifteen shelled domes decorated with frescoes, making for an impressive theatrical effect. In the attic space, tie-beams attached to the main beams support the domes as separate structures applied to the main vault. The twelve bays along the sides are elaborate and rich in architectural fantasy and ornament, while the three central bays appear as skylights filled with allegorical figures imbued with genealogical pride. The technique deployed in Palazzo Gangi's gallery vault goes back to Bibiena's stage sets and to the prodigious perspective of the allegorical main vault by Andrea Pozzo of the Jesuit church of Saint Ignatius in Rome. The trompe-l'oeil decoration of the twelve external canopy structures is probably the work of Gaspare Fumagalli, the leading artist of this genre active in Palermo at the time. The three central allegorical frescos may be the work of another hand, possibly that of Gaspare Serenario, one of the finest fresco painters of the mid-eighteenth century. All the same, the delicate hues point to the late eighteenth century rather than to an artist still attached to the warm fields of color and drapery of the High Baroque.

The floor of the gallery features depictions of the labors of Hercules. Experts believe it was made in Naples, where majolica manufactories were especially valued for the hard, uniform tiles they produced. We have documentation that Neapolitan manufactories often worked to designs by the Architects of the Senate, in this case probably Gigante himself. He probably also designed the Venetian-style wood panelling. The original furniture—console tables, chairs, and sofas—was lost in 1823 when the Valguarneras were forced to abandon the palace, as a result of which the furniture now in

the palace dates from the time of Napoleon III, and was built to order for the Cavaliere Giuseppe Mantegna, as were the Murano "Ca' Rezzonico" chandeliers. In contrast, the furniture of the two *poudreuses*, or dressing tables in the powder rooms on the far end of the gallery, giving on to the Piazza Santa Cecilia, date from the eighteenth century.

The second major project in the eighteenth century was the construction of the monumental staircase, also attributed to Gigante, despite documentation of the presence between 1759 and 1762 of the architect Mariano Sucameli, a less important figure than Gigante. In his thorough and detailed essay on the palace, Stefano Piazza asserts that, given the importance of the project, the monumental staircase should be attributed to Gigante, who had an ongoing relationship with Pietro Valguarnera thanks to the villa in Bagheria. The influence of Ferdinando Galli Bibiena could have come about through a collection of twenty-three prints entitled *Delizie farnesiane di Colorno* dating from 1723. The print entitled *Atrio all'ingresso del giardino* features a double-ramp structure that stands at an angle to the building, quite similar to the staircase in the palace. But it should be kept in mind that this sort of theatrical virtuosity was among the chief interests of Giovanni Biagio Amico, as seen both in his *L'Architetto pratico* and in the buildings that he constructed in Trapani. The Neapolitan influence in the design of the monumental staircase pointed out by Anthony Blunt or the Emilian influence noted by Anna Maria Matteucci are, more than anything else, merely indications of the arrival of the Rococo style even in far-flung Sicily.

Prince Pietro Valguarnera died in 1779. In his last will and testament, drawn up in 1768, he dictated: "I expressly command that my wife the Princess shall never have, for whatever reason, however justifiable, even the slightest liberty to change, in part or in whole, the design of the Great House that I newly rebuilt, and in which I now live, nor the form in which it currently exists, and the same thing shall apply to the Casina, or house, in Bagheria." The prince was proudly proclaiming that he was responsible for the two houses to which he had devoted his entire life, and decreeing that they be preserved as he had built them. Pietro's son Giuseppe Emanuele was his sole heir. The last quarter of the century had brought the Louis XVI style to Palermo. The scrollwork and curves of rocaille ornamentation began to yield to the straight lines of a classicist approach, and that style would lead, in turn, to the renovation of the interiors in the three antechambers that link the entry hall to the ballroom.

Giuseppe Emanuele commissioned Giovan Battista Cascione Vaccarini to modify parts of the palace and of the villa in Bagheria, bringing them into line with the new Louis XVI style. Construction on the Reggia, the royal palace at Caserta, was well underway, and the façades of many of Palermo's palaces were redesigned, in keeping with the classicism of Vanvitelli. The Palazzo Gangi's façades as well as the present-

The square-shaped ballroom is part of the glorious renovation of the interior decoration from 1750 to 1880. The beautiful tiled floor with battle scenes from a Sicilian manufactory and the vault decoration are pure mid-eighteenth century. The central vault fresco (opposite) is presumably a late work by Gaspare Serenario, the greatest Sicilian fresco painter of the eighteenth century. The fresco is enhanced by a frame of high stucco relief. The ballroom has direct access to the great terrace on the back of the palace. The southwest light filtering through the blinds or the late afternoon light and blue sky passing through the windows are among the special charms of Palermo's southern palaces. (Above) The Princess Giulia with her first two children, Stefanina—who was to bring the palace into the Vanni Calvello family—and her brother Benedetto.

day configuration of the terrace were both based on new architectural principles. Cascione Vaccarini also modified the panelling and the decoration over the doors in the ballroom and the adjoining antechambers. The team of decorators at this point included artists working at the end of the eighteenth century in the major villas of Bagheria and Palermo. Among the painters working here, we should mention Giuseppe Velasco—the Velázquez of Sicily, as he is still remembered in Palermo—a latter-day provincial Mengs, who painted the decoration over the doors of the ballroom. Alongside his work we see the more delicate brushstrokes of Elia Interguglielmi. Also present were Eugenio Fumagalli, the son of Gaspare Fumagalli, and the stucco artist Gaspare Firriolo. This same team was responsible for the decoration of the Villa Trabia in Bagheria.

The eighteenth-century floors were preserved, and we should mention in particular those of the ballroom with battle scenes, which Guido Donatone attributes to a Sicilian manufactory. The most successful project designed in the new Louis XVI style was the dining room. The idea of a special room in which to dine only became widespread during the late eighteenth century. The room's oval shape and elegant paneling must have once been the setting for a number of Louis XVI chairs and console tables, but these vanished, along with most of the original furnishings, in the earthquake of 1823. The Mantegnas replaced them with credenzas and chairs of the turn of the century. In their evocation of past and present these appear to be the work of a skilled designer, possibly Ernesto Basile, the architect responsible for the twentieth-century renewal of the palace. The vaulted ceiling features a fresco, *Psyche Ushered into Olympus by Mercury*, often attributed to Velasco but more likely the work of Elia Interguglielmi, that fits nicely into the setting of classically inspired panels. The Valguarnera coat-of-arms on the majolica tile floor has been attributed by Guido Donatone to a Neapolitan manufactory. The ceremonial bedroom of Prince Giuseppe Emanuele also reflects the "modern" idea of setting aside a room for a certain living function, an imported notion that did not take root in Sicily until the second half of the eighteenth century.

Prince Giuseppe Emanuele died in 1819 and was succeeded by his son Pietro. Pietro's father and grandfather had financed their building program with proceeds from public office. Pietro, the husband and uncle of the deaf-mute Marianna, had been one of the high officials of the court of Victor Amedeus of Savoy, who became king of Sicily following the Treaty of Utrecht. His son Giuseppe Emanuele had also served as

The library of Palazzo Gangi (above) has been built in what was the bedroom of Prince Pietro Emanuele, and occupies the antechamber and the alcove space where his bed had been. It is a space of memories filled with signed and framed portrait photographs of relatives, the ladies of the family in beautiful and fanciful ballgowns. The family appears to have been a compact community. Spread around are photographs of the many relatives of Cavaliere Mantegna's offspring: the many Alliata cousins, the Lanza di Mazzarino, the Valguarnera di Niscemi, the Tasca d'Almerita. Daughters and granddaughters of Cavaliere Giuseppe Mantegna married into the highest ranks of Sicilian nobility, possibly due to very good dowries, funded by Mantegna's business success. The two Sicilian gentlemen (left), Prince Gabriele Alliata di Villafranca and his brother, were cousins of Giuseppe Mantegna, Prince of Gangi. Due to their corpulence they were nicknamed "I tonni," or "the tunas."

Pretore, or Mayor of Palermo, and had held various other offices at court. But by 1819 the family's financial health was failing. The Valguarneras were no longer able to meet the costs of repairing the damage to the palace from the earthquake of 1823, soon fell behind on their payments for the lease, and their insolvency led to the confiscation of the palace by the Commenda della Magione.

Prince Pietro never married. His younger brother Girolamo married Giovanna Alliata, the daughter of his sister Agata Valguarnera and of Prince Giuseppe Alliata di Villafranca. The marriage was a sort of replay of that of Marianna Valguarnera to her uncle Pietro. Following the deaths of Girolamo, Prince of Gangi, in 1841, and then Pietro in 1855, the Valguarnera estate passed by female inheritance through Agata, sister of Pietro and Girolamo, to the Alliatas of Villafranca. Widowed in 1841, Giovanna Alliata in 1842 married Cavaliere Giuseppe Mantegna, a wealthy merchant and financier, who was born in the same year as his wife. She was allowed to keep and hand down to her descendants the princely Gangi title that her brother Pietro had bestowed upon her first husband Girolamo Valguarnera in 1838. As a consequence, in 1844 Palazzo Valguarnera Gangi was redeemed by Cavaliere Mantegna, and the purchase of the entire block was completed in 1847.

Giuseppe Mantegna then began work on the structural restoration of the palace, and he almost completely refurnished it, since the eighteenth-century furniture had largely been lost. Cavaliere Giuseppe's successor was Benedetto Mantegna, Prince of Gangi, who was in turn succeeded by his son Giuseppe. This Giuseppe commissioned a modest restoration from the renowned architect Ernesto Basile, the leading proponent of Art Nouveau in Sicily, and later asked him to install modern bathrooms, which had become the norm. A number of spaces for shops were created on the ground floor, the style of the façades was unified, and the façades were restored. The work, done under Basile's supervision, lasted from 1903 to 1927.

Prince Giuseppe Mantegna of Gangi left three children when he died, Stefania (Stefanina), Benedetto, and Giovanni. The two boys were handicapped, the transmission of certain genetic defects had been present in the Valguarnera family as far back as the deaf-mute Marianna Valguarnera, and took root in the male offspring of Cavaliere Mantegna. Benedetto and Giovanni Mantegna never married, and both palace and princely title were inherited by their sister Stefanina. In 1934, she married Vincenzo Vanni Calvello, Prince of San Vincenzo. Stefanina was remarkably beautiful, tall and with enchanting feline eyes. Vincenzo, her husband, was quite a handsome gentleman, and together they made a dazzling couple in Palermo's pre-war society. After their deaths, the palace and the title, by family agreement, were bequeathed to their second-oldest son, Giuseppe Vanni Calvello, Prince of Gangi. He carried out a number of structural and decorative restorations in the palace, where he now lives with his wife Carine.

The present Princess is a stately blond beauty from the Haute Savoie, whose life work has become the restoration and preservation of the Palazzo Gangi. Her mother was a friend of the prince, and they met when he came to visit her in France. The prince and princess spend their time between a chalet in Megeve, a seashore house near Palermo, and their Palermo palace. When they first moved in, the palace was in such ruinous condition that they were obliged to wash dishes in a bucket on the terrace, using a garden hose. Gone were the days of elegant dinner parties, whose menus and recipes are still kept in a drawer of the Empire-style console in the dining room. Wagner was no longer to be found writing in the library, and distinguished visitors from all over Europe no longer plotted to be invited to one of the many balls and receptions that took place in this most sumptuous of palaces. But the house is looking far better than it did before these Gangis took it on, and Carine works hard to raise the money that rapidly disappears in an endless program of improvements. She takes groups through the house by appointment, lectures knowledgeably, answers the invariably same questions as if she is hearing them the first time, and, depending on the time of day, offers her visitors either a coffee or a glass of champagne in the ballroom, where tables have been set with multi-colored sweet

The great Gallery of Mirrors (opposite) is what a Sicilian architect might imagine to be an equivalent of Versailles' Galerie des Glaces. The influence of Louis XIV's great royal building set the fashion for princely residential style all over Europe. From Germany to distant Sicily, Versailles and later Caserta became the models for palaces of the highest standard. But Sicily had its own say and this enchanted space is a world famous achievement of rocaille fantasy. The principal elements are the punctuated vault with its theatrical double-layered appearance, the admirable tiled floor depicting the Labors of Hercules, and the magnificent paneling. The ball scene of *The Leopard* revels in the charm of pale and delicate eighteenth-century gold patterns, in contrast to the shiny full yellow gilding of Victorian times. Originals and reproductions integrate here without apparent conflict, and beautiful late eighteenth-century Imari vases illustrate the Sicilian porcelain frenzy at its best. A parrot graces the tiled floor (above). Due to the pale bright green of their feathers, the parrot was one of the preferred themes in eighteenth-century Sicilian floor tile design. (Right) The present Princess Gangi in the gallery.

(Preceding pages) A stately console in the Gallery of Mirrors with a Louis XV clock and late eighteenth-century Imari vases, set against carved wood paneling with Ca' Rezzonico style appliques and refurbished rocaille furnishings. On the right, Marchesa Giulia Paternò di Spedalotto at the "Marie-Antoinette" ball standing in the Chinese cabinet or *poudreuse* off the mirror gallery. The two *poudreuse* cabinets (above and opposite) at the far end of the gallery are the absolute delight of the whole palace. Their magic is charming and discreet. Instead of the wide Neapolitan tiles of the gallery floor, here are smaller Sicilian ones showing an elaborate and rather thick ornamental pattern. The lacquer and the gilding of the paneling is enchanting, its delicate pastel colors invoking the age of *plaisir de vivre* the Marquis de Talleyrand remembered in Europe before the French Revolution of 1789. The aura of intimacy suggests the delightful masquerades that once took place in this restricted space.

Sicilian pastries or sandwiches, small tomatoes, and mozzarella balls. The family silver is laid out, carafes are filled with Marsala wine, and the house's butler, Giovanni, in a mustard-colored jacket, presides as elegantly as any Valguarnera footman used to in the family livery. Carine is very much the hostess, everybody forgets that they are paying for the privilege, and most look somewhat in awe. As soon as they leave, Giovanni washes the dishes before hosing down the terrace or fixing the electricity; the only maid goes back to sweeping the floors or polishing the silver and sets everything up for another imminent reception to raise badly needed funds. The house can also be rented for the evening, but there is no longer a vast kitchen presided over by a monsu (the Sicilian term for a French chef), and a caterer brings in everything.

There have been many paying visitors since Luchino Visconti made the palace famous in his 1963 film based on Lampedusa's novel *The Leopard*, and everybody still remembers the ball scene in which Claudia Cardinale, Burt Lancaster, Alain Delon, and Romolo Valli dance in the palace's beautiful ballroom to the accompaniment of an unknown waltz by Giuseppe Verdi.

PALAZZO SACCHETTI

A Cardinal's Palace on the Tiber

The Palazzo Sacchetti is the most Roman of palaces, owing to its location on the Via Giulia, illustrious history, and rich contents and decoration. Looking out over the Tiber, this imposing building is in the heart of Baroque Rome and but a few minutes walk from the monuments that figure in *Tosca*, Puccini's popular opera: Sant'Andrea della Valle, the Palazzo Farnese, and the Castel Sant'Angelo. The Vatican, too, is very close—just across the Tiber.

The Via Giulia, in its early days (left, bottom), served as a place for festivals, theatrical performances, jousting tournaments, even races of naked hunchbacks. In 1638, it was used for a lavish procession to honor the French Dauphin, who was to become Louis XIV. The local population followed these spectacles from the street while the aristocracy watched from their carriages or from the balconies and windows of their palaces. They could also follow boat races and processions on the Tiber from their gardens and riverside terraces (at least until the nineteenth century when a road, the Lungotevere, was laid out that separated houses and palaces from the river's edge). This festive character of the street has continued, and in summer the neighborhood is still filled with lights, spectacles, and throngs of Romans and tourists.

Many talented Florentines, who felt constrained at home by the power of the Medici, emigrated to Rome, and they were drawn to the neighborhood of the Via Giulia by the church of San Giovanni dei Fiorentini, the church of the Florentine's, which stands at the north end of the street. Various institutions such as the Consolato, founded by Pope Leo X in 1515, and the Confraternity of the Pietá di San Giovanni bound together such Florentines as the Ruspoli, Aldobrandini, Barberini, and Sachetti. They, in turn, befriended the likes of the Strozzi, Gaddi, and Ruccelai families, most of whom were talented bankers who saw great career possibilities in the Roman Curia and in the financial needs of the great city of Rome. This easy access to Rome's power structure is what impelled Giovanni Battista Sacchetti to leave Florence for the Eternal City in 1573. A talented merchant and banker, he quickly joined the Florentine inner circle, and between 1574 and 1601 Giovanni Battista was a powerful figure in Roman commerce, dealing in grain and other commodities, and enjoying close links to the papal court. He slowly and carefully used his skills to establish a new dynasty. In his last will and testament, he instructed his sons—Giulio, Giovanni, Marcello, Alessandro, and Matteo—to build a family chapel and monument in San Giovanni dei Fiorentini, thus officially planting the family's Roman roots on the Via Giulia. Five years after the death of their father, the young Sacchettis demonstrated

(Previous pages) The Sala dei Mappamondi by Francesco Salviati. The back elevation of the Palazzo Sacchetti is seen (above) in an eighteenth-century watercolor. The palace then had an embankment that ran down to the Tiber; this was filled in during the nineteenth century to make a road, the Lungotevere, that carries traffic along the riverbank. The lower part of the house's façade disappeared in the process and it now starts at the level of the garden (opposite), whose arch is still crowned by a giant Roman patrician head. The garden was the first in Rome to have oleander bushes, and displayed antiquities from the renowned Ceuli collection when that family occupied the palace. The front façade of the house on the Via Giulia (below) in a 1699 engraving by Giovanni Battista Falda is seen in a way that is unachievable on the rather narrow street. Here we can truly appreciate the harmony and proportion of classic architectural elements as used by Antonio da Sangallo the Younger, the most important architect in Europe after he was put in charge of St. Peter's.

Cardinal Giulio Sacchetti (right) as painted by his protégé Pietro da Cortona, one of the most fashionable artists in Rome thanks to his frescoes in the Palazzo Barberini. Giulio solidified the link between the Vatican states and his banking brothers, vastly increasing the family fortune and was a great art patron in the Medici tradition. The power of the Sacchettis in Rome is made palpable when entering the reception rooms on the piano nobile from a narrow corridor filled with ancient Roman marble portrait busts (above). In the distance can be seen, through a series of arches, the entrance to the Galleria (overleaf). This later addition overlooks the Tiber and is used by the present owners for receiving from eight to a hundred guests for lunch or dinner. It contains the only contemporaneous copies of parts of Michelangelo's

Sistine Ceiling, painted by Giacomo Rocca, as well as stained-glass windows, and an elaborate coffered ceiling with the Sacchetti arms. (Opposite) The palace's rooms are filled with sumptuous Roman Baroque carved and gilded eighteenth-century furniture.

their success and power by choosing no less than Giovanni Lanfranco for this important commission.

The most capable businessman of this new generation of Sacchettis was undoubtedly Marcello. Thanks to the protection of the powerful Barberini family and Pope Urban VII (who ascended to the papal throne in 1623), he gained control of the Vatican's depository and secret treasury, the treasury of Urbino, and the customs office in Ancona. With the vast profits from these assets, he started purchasing major estates outside Rome. He had multiple interests, and became a major patron of the arts. He was also a member of the scientific Accademia dei Lincei where he grew close to Galileo Galilei and Giovanni Battista Marino. In the 1640s, however, the commercial activities of this highly successful family slowed down as the Sacchetti sons now concentrated on the ecclesiastical career of their brother Giulio (left below). Calculating as all Florentines are, they knew that closer contacts with the rich and powerful Vatican state through high position in Rome could only be good for business. After studying law at the University of Pisa, Giulio became one of the prelates of Pope Paul V and enjoyed the protection of Cardinal Carlo de Medici and the friendship of Francesco Barberini. In 1624, Pope Urban VII appointed him Nuncio to King Philip IV of Spain, a tricky post since he had to mediate between France and Spain in order to prevent war in Valtellina, where the Vatican had territorial interests. When war broke out there despite his efforts, he was appointed commissioner of the papal forces.

He remained in Spain for three years, and toward the end of his stay was made a Cardinal. He returned to Rome where his excellent work and piety made him *papabile*—a candidate for the papacy—on two occasions. It was in 1649, exactly midway between two papal elections, that the Sacchettis purchased the splendid house on the Via Giulia, where they still live, an appropriate Roman residence for a family that reigned over *orbis et urbis*. This date, in many ways, marked the apogee of the family as businessmen, estate owners, powers in the Papal States, art collectors, and patrons. The purchase of the house that would thereafter be known as the Palazzo Sacchetti, perhaps brought them bad luck that ended in financial decline. Or, it was hubris that overextended the family during several financial crises, while Urban VIII lost interest in the family's financial welfare. He may have felt that the family's interest had changed from making money to making popes. There was the sudden unpleasant possibility of going from shirtsleeves to shirtsleeves in three generations. The Sacchettis had spent too much money and had not managed their country properties well, but at least these were so grand that nobody could have felt that they were under-housed. First came the Villa Castelfusano in Ostia near Rome, designed and decorated between 1628 and 1629 as a fortified villa by their protégé Pietro da Cortona in collaboration with Andrea Sacchi.

No sooner was it finished than Giovanni Battista started work on a folly near a small house he had bought from Pius V in the Valle dell'Inferno. He called on Pietro da Cortona once more, and the result was one of the most beautiful buildings of the period, more a stage set than a house—the Villa del Pigneto. This eventually became an abandoned ruin that was recorded by such great *vedute* painters Gaspar van Wittel (known also as Vanvitelli) and Hubert Robert. Finally, there was the Villa Ruffinella in Frascati, a favored and very expensive vacation spot for the Roman aristocracy, the Curia, and the papal court. In the late eighteenthth century, this estate passed through the hands of Lucien Bonaparte, Marina of Savoy, and Cristina de Bourbon, all of whom were used to the finest things in life.

The palace the Sacchettis bought on the Via Giulia must have cost them a great fortune. It was designed by the renowned Roman architect Antonio da Sangallo the Younger for his own use. He was born in 1485, and had apprenticed with his uncles Giuliano and Antonio before becoming an assistant to Bramante himself. In 1520, he replaced Raphael at St. Peter's, becoming the most important architect in Europe and the favorite designer of the rising, powerful Roman aristocracy. Sangallo thought a great deal about building palaces, and knew that what he built for himself would be carefully watched by prospective clients—and so he provided for himself only the best. Architects at the time were also, to a degree, real estate promoters and developers, and Sangallo had actively collected land in this part of town, particularly on the Villa Giulia, for decades. In 1543, he consolidated various plots, drew up plans, and started building, proudly declaring on the façade of his palace that this was "Domus Antonii Sangalli Architecti MDXLIII," an inscription that is still there. Unfortunately, this was never to be since Sangallo died in 1546 before the building was completed. There were problems with the estate after his wife, the daughter of a Florentine patrician who he had married some twenty years earlier, and her second husband falsified papers in order to inherit everything. So it is unlikely that work on the palace proceeded much after the architect's death. These problems were resolved only in 1549, and in 1552 Sangallo's son Orazio sold the house to Cardinal Giovanni Ricci. This Prince of the Church was born in Montepulciano in 1497, and made his career as a secretary to and diplomat for Pope Paul III. He bought Sangallo's palace the very year he was made a cardinal by Giulio III—a purchase made necessary by the grand lifestyle incumbent upon a man of such position. Being a cardinal involved holding audiences, receiving members of his own as well the papal court, entertaining the best of Roman society and grandees visiting the Vatican, and conveying the grandeur and importance of the Holy See.

There is evidence that in 1552 floors were being laid in what is now the Ricci Palace, and generally (although there is current disagreement) it is thought that Francesco Salviati started work on the renowned Winter Gallery frescoes of the palace

The Sacchettis now occupy only one floor of the palace; the others are rented out as apartments or offices. Their apartment is a series of salons laid out in three interconnecting and open *defilés* (above). Despite the formality of the layout, the palace is very much a family home. The Stanza di Ulisse (above) is generally used to gather before dinner while the Stanza della Stagione (opposite and overleaf) has been made into a cozy library filled with books on art, history, and science belonging to the present Marchese. In the corner of the room by the window, chess, backgammon, and card games are played on quiet evenings. The sun streams through the windows into all these rooms, constantly changing the ambience and lighting up the quite unusually patterned terracotta floors.

that same year. The Tuscan Cardinal Ricci belonged to the Florentine power group that was centered in the Via Giulia church of the Florentines, and he hired Nanni di Baccio Bigio to finish his new palace in the princely style he required. The house became grander than what Sangallo had planned, but it would seem evident from the chronology that the structure is fully attributable to Sangallo rather than to Baccio Biggio, a faithful adherent of the Sangallo style. Soon, Ricci bought an adjacent house owned by the Masari brothers and, by incorporating that into the palace, he created additional rooms. Cardinal Ricci also added a magnificent long gallery overlooking the Tiber (pages 138–139). He was so pleased by everything that Baccio Biggi had done that he commissioned him to design and decorate his apartments in the Vatican as well as to remodel his villa outside the city (known today as the Villa Medici and home to the French Academy in Rome).

In 1576, ownership of the Via Giulia palace passed to the Ceuli family, rich bankers from Pisa who moved to Rome. They embellished their new palace with 273 marble antiquities that would later be transferred to the Vatican Museums. The Ceuli decorated Ricci's long gallery overlooking the Tiber with copies of some of the frescoes by Michelangelo in the Sistine Chapel. They developed the large Renaissance garden with its low, spouting fountain, trimmed boxwood hedges, lush meridional trees, Roman statues, and planted parterres overflowing with fragrant white flowers set amidst raked gravel pathways. This was the first garden in Rome to make extensive use of oleander. At the end of the garden, they added the large Ninfea crowned by a gigantic Roman patrician head. Having achieved its final form, this Renaissance masterpiece would then be sold to the Sacchetti family in 1649 in order to give their own Cardinal Giulio a palace worthy of his position.

During the Renaissance, art and power were closely related—starting, of course, with the Medicis in Florence, undoubtedly history's most astonishing patrons and collectors. For the Sacchettis, who would follow the Medici example, art patronage and collecting were a means of demonstrating their integration into Roman society, of impressing their clients with the family's wealth and power, and proving that they were interested in the finer things of life. The purchase of the Via Giulia palace allowed Marcello and his brothers to display their collection—then numbering more than seven hundred paintings, magnificent Baroque furniture, and a *guardaroba* full of treasures—in a truly sumptuous setting. Their closest protégé was Pietro da Cortona, a leading architect and painter of the Baroque period, who was famous for his ceiling in the Barberini Palace in Rome and frescoes for the Palazzo Pitti in Florence. He designed and frescoed the Sacchetti Villa di Castelfusano, painted many family portraits, and made second versions for the family of such renowned works as Raphael's *Galatea*, and Titian's *Virgin and Child with Saints Catherine and John the Baptist*. The Sacchettis commissioned fifteen major

(Opposite) The Stanza de Ulisse is one of the most sumptuously refurbished rooms in the palace and conveys to guests the importance of the Sacchetti family as art collectors even after having sold 187 of their paintings in 1748 to create the core of the Pinacoteca Capitolina on the Campidoglio. Against the far wall is Vincenzo Campi's *Matrimony in the House of the Pharisee*. Pierre Subleyras' *Mystic Marriage of Saint Catherine* now hangs in another salon (above). A pair of magnificent

Roman Baroque gilded consoles (overleaf) are embellished by Chinese Imari porcelain vases and Roman clocks. This is the room where guests generally gather for coffee (below). Between the windows is an eighteenth-century Roman secretaire (overleaf, right).

(Below) The Marchesa Sacchetti is seated by one of the great globes by Coronelli in the Sala dei Mappamondi. She is Brazilian born, she is one of Rome's great hostesses, and she bore the responsibility of refurbishing and redecorating her husband's palace while keeping its Renaissance character. She did this together with the Roman decorator Federico Forquet, and organizes many large and small receptions for friends and for charity. Her husband served as Governor General of the Vatican for many years before his retirement.

paintings from Cortona including *The Battle of Alexander and Darius* and *The Rape of the Sabines*. They were among the early patrons of Simon Vouet and Nicolas Poussin when both were studying in Rome, and, according to family inventories, owned fine paintings by Guercino, Garofalo, Vanvitelli, and Mantegna. In 1748, pursuant to the decline in the family's immense fortune, they sold 178 paintings to the gallery on Rome's Campidoglio, which became the basis of what is known today as the Pinacoteca Capitolina. This transaction was particularly important as a counterbalance to the hemorrhage of paintings from Italy to Britain owing to the Grand Tour, its grand tourists and their appetite for souvenirs. The sale of country estates followed the sale of paintings, but the family continued to play important roles at the Vatican, and to remain closely linked to the papacy.

The present head of the family, Giulio Sacchetti, like his predecessors, is one of the four Marchesi del Baldacchino who are allowed to carry a baldachin over the pope during important processions at the Vatican. The other hereditary families so honored are the Theodolis, Serottis, and Costa Guttis. These marchesi are, of course, prominent members of Rome's "black aristocracy," so called because their titles came from the Vatican, rather than members of the "white aristocracy" enno-

for reproduction rights to these masterpieces. The restoration revealed astonishing, strange Mannerist colors from under centuries of soot that had risen from candles below and from the application of glues and varnishes to the stucco in order to clarify the frescos. The restoration of Michelangelo's frescoes endured severe but misguided criticism by a few art historians more interested in self-promotion than in finally, properly seeing the work itself.

The Sacchetti palace has been continuously inhabited by family members from the mid-seventeenth century to today, although the Sacchettis now only occupy the *piano nobile*, or main floor, which has a dozen large reception rooms (of which one is a guest bedroom) and a wing at the back. This wing has been transformed into family living quarters with a Renaissance study, a few bedrooms, a large kitchen and pantry, and a few servants' rooms. The other floors of the immense palace are rented out as offices or small flats. When Giulio, the present marchese, married for the second time, he asked his wife, Giovanna, to redecorate the house in a way that would project its splendor, keep its very Roman character, and yet be completely livable. In other words, he wanted a place where the family could wander around in sweaters, read, watch TV, and still entertain large and small groups of their friends in grand style. The Brazilian-born marchesa told her husband that she had no experience redecorating Roman palaces, and he put her in the hands of a renowned, highly civilized, and knowledgeable Roman interior designer, Federico Forquet, who had just redecorated the *piano nobile* of Rome's Palazzo Altieri, helped with the decoration of Prince Moritz of Hesse's Schloss Wolfsgarten, and worked closely with Marella Agnelli on several of her houses. The Sacchetti refurbishing started in the 1980s and Federico, with Giovanna's collaboration, removed many nineteenth-century additions—including large, florid Venetian-glass chandeliers—rewired the entire apartment, and made the wonderful stucco and fresco friezes in every room look as if they were illuminated by candlelight.

All the floors are covered in early nineteenth-century terracotta tiles in shades of deep brown, black, and gray. Many of these floors had been replaced by marble in the nineteenth century, which was grand and traditional but less sophisticated. By removing the marble and putting down ceramic tiles, all the rooms gained a warmth and variety of shading quite different from that of any palace in Rome. When the sun pours through the large windows, the rooms now seem to glow. Forquet found subtle wall coverings, which were either stenciled or patterned, and sumptuous fabrics of the highest quality to set off the Sacchetti coats of arms that are appliquéd in shades of gold onto crimson drapes, and can be drawn across the double doorways separating the different salons. A secret treasure for Giovanna and Federico was a closet they found in the palace filled with samples of old material. While decorating, they combed the antique stores of Rome to find

bled by Italy's kings who were installed only after the unification of the nation by Garibaldi in 1861. The Marchesi del Baldacchino are also allowed to display a baldachin in their houses, as the Sacchettis do in the corridor to their apartments. More important, Giulio Sacchetti was appointed Governor General of the Vatican in 1964, a special position created by Pope Paul VI after the dissolution of the papal court. The Governor General is responsible for the vast bureaucracy that controls all of the nonreligious activity of the Vatican state. This encompasses everything from providing electricity to being responsible for art and museums. Extremely tall, distinguished, handsome, and efficient, the marchese performed duties that included greeting, in white tie and decorations, all official guests on behalf of the pope (page 154), leading them and their families into his presence, and staying with them during their audience. A room in the Sacchetti palace is devoted to photographs of these occasions, with the marchese receiving people like the emperor of Japan and the president of the United States.

Among Giulio Sacchetti's great accomplishments was commissioning and supervising the restoration of Michelangelo's Sistine Chapel ceiling and *Last Judgment*, and negotiating the funding of all this work by Japan's NHK Television in return

The Stanza dei Fatti Mitologici, recently redecorated by Federico Forquet, is where guests are taken for an aperitivo before lunch. Forquet worked on the Palazzo Sacchetti for nearly twenty years. "My inspiring purpose," he says, "was based on the desire to create the illusion that nothing new had been introduced to disturb the continuity of the palace's particular style." The unusual combination of blue upholstered chairs and walls with crimson curtains could seem novel, yet it is in perfect harmony with the umber, checkered terracotta floor. Roman paintings hang here, and the gold and crimson drape becomes

the Sacchetti coat of arms when pulled across the marble doorframe. Through the doorway is the Stanza di Tobia (overleaf), in fact an antechamber to the recessed family chapel that has a splendid cupola frescoed by Agostino Ciampelli. The crucifix would seem at cross purposes with the leering satyrs on the decorative frieze.

Baroque furniture and objets d'art to supplement the fine things that had remained in the palace.

The Palazzo Sacchetti is not open to the public, although the family welcomes scholars to study the family archives and they allow a few guided visits every year for serious groups. Occasionally they host large dinners for major charities or museums such as the Museum of Modern Art in New York or the Israel Museum in Jerusalem. Giovanna is a very skilled and welcoming hostess and likes nothing more than receiving the many interesting people who are always visiting Rome, and filling her house with Italian and foreign friends. Needless to say, her invitations are coveted and her large dinners and smaller lunches are very much what one would expect in the home of Roman grandees. Among her guests are the descendents of the same families that the Sacchettis felt they had to know when they emigrated from Florence in the fifteenth century: the Doria, Colonna, Borghese, Aldobrandini, and Boncampagni families. Princes of the Church were regular visitors when Giulio was Governor of the Vatican, and ambassadors consider a meal at the Palazzo Sacchetti as essential as a visit to the Quirinale Palace. Guests include fashion figures such as Valentino and his partner, Gian Carlo Giametti, Cristina Pucci, Giorgio Armani, Kenneth Lane, and various members of the Ferragamo family. There are also visits from renowned art collectors like the Rothschilds and Jayne Wrightsman, who enjoy talking to leading scholars and art historians, and people from la dolce vita such as Cinecittá film producer Roberto Haggiag, or Andrea Dotti, the husband of the late Audrey Hepburn

A first impression of the palace is a bit forbidding. The building seems enormous and fortresslike on the narrow Via Giulia, and this is accentuated by the heavy bars on the ground-floor windows. Once through the door, however, one enters the magnificent courtyard, offering a display by Sangallo of the Renaissance architectural vocabulary in stone and marble that shows his taste and knowledge. A fairly narrow and dark stone staircase, embellished by Roman sarcophagi, ascends to the *piano nobile*, where the visitor enters the family apartments through a vaulted corridor. One is immediately impressed by the family's grandeur: at the far end is the crimson and gold family coat of arms setting off a huge polished alabaster vase on a marble base, to the right is the Marchese's baldachin, to the left rows of portraits of Roman patricians and, through marble arches, there is a view of the long gallery on the Tiber. Footmen guide you along towards the Stanza di Marmitta, where the hosts await their guests. This is the first room that begins to convey the importance of the family collections with its gilded Baroque furniture, a wonderful, large canvas by Pierre Subleyras of the Marriage of Saint Catherine, a large seventeenth-century carved unicorn's head that supports a narwhal tusk (in its day identified as belonging to the unicorn), Diego Velázquez's portraits of

King Felipe IV and Isabella de Bourbon, and Giambologna's bronze Mercury.

This is the room where guests at a small party first congregate and chat until led to one of the nearby salons by the hostess, or it is the place they are greeted by their hosts at a large gathering before passing freely into the interconnecting *defilé* of rooms of state to enjoy drinks served by butlers in livery embellished by gold buttons with the family arms. The Stanza di Marmitta, like the other salons, has coffered stucco ceilings and a broad frieze with frescoes inset into a stucco framework. Here, the paintings are of landscapes, while in the other rooms, they are linked to a specific figure such as Romulus, Ulysses, Tobias, or Solomon. These frescoes, created in the 1550s, are not among the most important in Rome, but they reflect the influence of Raphael's loggia in the Vatican, of Primaticcio and Perino del Vaga. They also show the influence of Mannerism in Fontainebleau thanks to Ponsio Jacquio, who was in charge of this fresco project, and for which he engaged other talented painters such as Pellegrino Bolognese and Marco Marchetti.

In sequence, the rooms passed through by guests from the Stanza di Marmitta are as follows: the Stanza di Romolo, a large and comfortable living room with a renowned portrait of Cardinal Giulio by Pietro da Cortona; the Stanza delle Stagione (page 142–143), Giulio Sacchetti's book-filled library; the damask-walled Stanza di Ulisse (page 144) with important Flemish paintings, and large, carved, and gilded Roman eighteenth-century wood consoles that set off wonderful timepieces and bronze-mounted Chinese porcelain vases; the very small Stanza di Mosè, a room at the corner of the house, filled with light and a collection of Raphaelesque watercolors, that acts as a sort of antechamber to a further *défilé* of rooms. These rooms are the Stanza dei Fatti Mitologici (pages 148–149), which Forquet decorated in subtle shades of pale blue damask with crimson curtains; the sedate Stanza di Tobia (pages 150–151), followed by the small family chapel with its elaborate domed ceiling with frescoes attributed to Agostini Ciampelli and a Resurrection of Christ; and then the Stanza di Salomone, which leads into the great masterpiece of the palace and one of the most spectacular sights in all of Europe, the Sala dei Mappamondi—entirely frescoed by Francesco Salviati (pages 152, 153). On the other side of the Salviati room is the Stanza di Alessandro, followed by the Stanza di Annibale, which is essentially a gallery of family portraits. Giovanna's favorite rooms for conversation, possibly because they have comfortable sofas and armchairs, are the Stanza di Romolo, the Stanza di Ulisse, which serves as the main drawing room where even large groups can gather in the evening for coffee, and the smaller, even more opulent Stanza di Fatti Mitologici. For lunching or dining she uses the Galleria, and for extremely festive occasions she fills the Sala dei Mappamondi with up to 120 people, seated at tables of ten. Anybody who has the good fortune to dine by candlelight

The Sala dei Mappamondi by Francesco Salviati is not only the highlight of the Sacchetti Palace, but also one of the most astonishing works of art in all Rome. It is the quintessence of the Mannerist style that developed at the end of the High Renaissance. According to the painter and historian Giorgio Vasari, Salviati worked here in a veritable frenzy of creativity. There is a consensus that these frescoes were finished around 1554, and the room was first known as the Winter Audience Room when the palace was occupied by Cardinal Ricci. When the Sacchettis purchased the palace, they placed here two important globes giving the room its new name. While the panels of the room can be identified, nobody agrees on the all-encompassing meaning of this remarkable creation. A marble bust of Cardinal Giulio Sacchetti presides here, and a naked male figure representing the allegory of sleep (above) was inspired by Michelangelo's ignudi on the Sistine ceiling. Sleep is draped over a window frame, and looks as if he were about to drop onto the floor below.

in the middle of Salviati's masterpiece must keep pinching himself in order to know that it is not a dream.

The Galleria's decorative program operates on three levels (pages 138–139). On the first are plaster casts of antique figures set into niches that alternate with large windows that flood the room with light. Above that, the second level consists of plaster copies of patrician portraits inset into gilded roundels that alternate with copies of Sibyls and Prophets from Michelangelo's Sistine Chapel. The third or topmost level consists of scenes from the Sistine ceiling flanked by plaster figures of naked white youths, some draped in gold robes. This room is a sort of dress rehearsal for what the Carracci were later going to produce in the nearby Palazzo Farnese. The frescoes are by the Roman artist Giacomo Rocca, and this entire decoration was most probably commissioned by the Ceuli family soon after they bought the palace. The frescoes are not of extraordinary quality, but they are the only extant, literal copies of Michelangelo's masterpiece made in the century in which the originals were created. One can imagine Tiberio Ceuli asking Rocca to reproduce in his own house a work he greatly admired, and embellishing it with dazzling decoration. There are also two frescoes on the second level by Pietro da Cortona, which have no relation at all to the scheme, and were certainly a later Sacchetti contribution. In the center of the long room is an Empire table with Valadier candelabras that can seat sixteen, and off both ends of the table are rather rare white and gold Empire free-standing consoles that display the family porcelain, and are used for buffets. Toward the entrance door that leads from the Stanza di

Marmitta is a cozy table for eight. If the gallery is not high art it is certainly high decoration and a wonderful setting for a dinner party!

However, nobody could say that the Sala dei Mappamondi (pages 152–153) is not high art or a perfect example of the anxiety and illusion of Mannerist art. Salviati was famous for his frescoes in the Palazzo Pitti in Florence and at the Palazzo Farnese, and had worked over a period of twenty years in Fontainebleau. This great hall is named for two large, seventeenth-century globes that have always been in the possession of the Sacchetti family and are placed in the center, but it has also been known as the Winter Audience Room. The globes, signed by Padre Vincenzo Coronelli, were made in 1688, and represent the world as it was then known. The frescoes are lit by large windows on two levels, and the viewer is constantly challenged to discern between reality and illusion, between two dimensions and three, between actual Roman marbles set into seashells over the doors and painted sculptural images. At the very top of the walls, where they meet the ceiling, Salviati actually carries the fresco into three dimensions—a demonstration of the greatest virtuosity. He creates the illusion that larger panels, such as the *Death of Saul* or the *Death of Absalom*, are actually framed and hanging from Ionic marble columns. He seats large, naked, and contorted grisaille figures on top of these frames, as if their feet are flopping into the air. Figures of naked men, inspired by Michelangelo's nudes, recline across the frames of the tall windows at one end of the great room. The influence of Michelangelo's Sistine ceiling, painted nearly a half century earlier, is seen everywhere here, but Salviati has transformed High Renaissance balance and harmony into Mannerist confusion and detail. In the large panels, there are literally hundreds of bodies, and the profusion of wreaths, flowers, and fruit is overwhelming and purposely confusing, as is any attempt to explain the allegories. After these frescos were completed, Salviati left for France and when he returned to Rome many years later his great ambition was to paint the Sala Regia in the Vatican. Michelangelo successfully conspired with the painter Daniele di Volterra to thwart him, and Salviati tragically produced nothing in his late years.

When leaving the Sacchetti house after a wonderful evening of warm hospitality and good conversation, the guests think how astonishing it is that so much art and history are still in private hands. Giovanna Sacchetti is fond of saying that it is both a privilege to own the palace and an obligation to allow others to enjoy it, and she is a master of the art of hospitality.

The present Marchese Sacchetti was, for many years, Governor General of the Vatican, and one of his many duties was greeting heads of state on their visits to the Pope and accompanying them during their audience. He is seen (left) welcoming the emperor of Japan and other dignitaries. (Opposite) The Marchese's study is in a wing at the back of the house that also has two bedrooms and bathrooms and a corridor filled with family souvenirs. It has the clutter of a home lived in by two busy people. The walnut bookshelves and busts of writers and philosophers are the reflection of a Florentine humanist.

SCHLOSS ST. EMMERAM

(Previous pages) The bedroom of
the Princess Margerete (1870–1955)
in the south wing of the castle.
Her state funeral (left),
in St. Emmeram's rococo church
(opposite), followed an unchanging
procession of family ritual.
Her crowned bier was flanked by
gold-liveried footmen and the family
coats of arms were prominently
displayed in the nave and on the
high altar. Several thousand loyal
Regensburgers followed the funeral
procession when the princess's
remains were borne in state to the
family mausoleum in the center
of the original medieval Benedictine
cloister (above), which dates back
to the eighth century. The interior
of St. Emmeram's church
(1731–1733) is a fine example
of Bavarian rococo architecture
by the Asam brothers. The original
monastery was the burial site
of a revered saint, the Franconian
Bishop Emmeram who was
murdered at the instigation of his
son. In the twelfth century, the
monastery was seriously damaged
in a fire but much remains of
the original sculpture and frescoes.
It was secularized in 1810 when
it became part of the Thurn und
Taxis castle.

A Postal Empire in Bavaria

Few families maintained the high level and intensity of private
splendor as long as the late Prince Johannes von Thurn und
Taxis, who died in 1990. He left behind an incredibly compli-
cated estate in the hands of a group of professional managers
he had personally selected, but whose competence to run what
was left of the family fortune was, quite rightly, contested in
court by his widow, the equally aristocratic Princess Maria
Gloria von Schönburg-Glachau. The couple had lived happily
together in Schloss St. Emmeram, a former monastery in the
heart of Bavaria's ancient city of Regensburg, with their three
children: Prince Albert II, heir to the princely title and fortune;
Princess Maria Theresia, a filmmaker; and Princess Elisabeth,
who is at present working at an art gallery in New York City.
The Schloss is the largest private home in Europe still kept up
by a princely family. Princess Gloria, who lives there part of
the year, as do her children when they return home, remembers with a certain nostalgia and little regret the palmy days
when Prince Johannes employed two hundred people to work
in his castle, including ten footmen who dressed on gala occasions in the blue family livery of knee breeches, buckled shoes,
powdered wigs, as well as swords. They still appear occasionally, although as extras hired for special occasions, such as
hunting weekends. "Now my son does the inviting," says
Princess Gloria, "but I organize it. I see all the friends of the
young generation, and they are perfect ladies and gentlemen.
It is really beautiful for me to be able to do this for my children and see what the next generation is up to."
St. Emmeram has about ten guest bedrooms that are strung
along a broad corridor—rather like that of a palace hotel—in
Princess Gloria's wing. And there are another ten guest rooms
in the north wing. The most luxurious was built for the late
Princess Margarete (1870–1955), and it was last slept in by
the King of Spain, when he visited the schloss (preceding
pages). "I now have a personal staff of two, and there are sixteen people in all working in the castle on maintenance, secu-
rity, and so forth. Our personal staff alone used to be ten
people, including three butlers, three in the kitchen, nannies,
and valets. I stopped all that," says the bright and still beautiful princess. The chef went off to run a successful first class
restaurant, which was what St. Emmeram often resembled in
the prince's heyday. Princess Gloria now mostly eats with her
children in a modern, cozy, and elegant kitchen, where the kids
whip up pasta and pizza while they watch TV with their
mother and friends. One maid takes care of everybody, but
then the princess also has a flat in Paris and another in Rome,
where she sees a great deal of the present Pope—the former

Cardinal Joseph Ratzinger of Regensburg. And the princess recently built a house on a beach in Kenya where she goes with her extended family in the winter. They also spend some time at the enormous Schloss Taxis, between Stuttgart and Ulm, on Lake Starnberg, although most of that stately pile has become an old people's home run by the local government. And finally, there is an enchanting nineteenth-century hunting lodge that was copied from a Romanoff dacha where the late Prince Johannes's father had stayed with the Russian Emperor. Prince Johannes once said, "When you have as many castles as the Thurn und Taxis—we had eighteen in the family at one time—you tend not to worry if you happen to lose a few. So, I tell my children, 'we still have two left for each of you, so please don't grumble about the past.'"

Having a small staff by no means prevents Gloria from organizing beautiful parties in the dining room of her wing, such as the annual Christmas dinner (pages 180–181), more intimate lunches or dinners in the plush south wing (page 169), and larger, more formal dinners during the shooting parties in the Green Dining Room of the north wing. Its walls are covered with priceless seventeenth-century Gobelin tapestries showing the family in battle during the early days of its history in Italy. In the summer, the princess invites her friends to join thousands

The inner courtyard of St. Emmeram (right) is the largest of any German princely residence. The grandest room of the house is the Festsaal, or Ballroom (opposite), which was designed by the Munich architect Max Schultze and finished in 1891. Much of the decoration came from the family palace in Frankfurt and the double-height ceiling allowed paneling to be transferred intact, rather than cut down to size as in other rooms. The elaborate eighteenth-century stove is in blue faience and bronze gilt, and above it is the musicians' gallery. (Above) The house chapel in the same wing is decorated in Venetian Renaissance style, and was finished in 1876. Above the altar is a devotional image of Christ by the late-period Nazarene painter, Ernst Deger, and the stained-glass windows show coats of arms of various royal families into which the Thurn und Taxis had married. In 1893, Prince Albert incorporated the bedroom in which his mother died into this chapel.
(Overleaf) The Library of St. Emmeram was designed by the Linz architect Johann Michael

Prunner. When the Thurn und Taxis family moved in, they painted over splendid frescoes by the renowned Cosmas Damian Asam in 1737. A note describing them by one of the monks at St. Emmeram was found in the library, alerting the reigning prince to the hidden masterpiece. He had the ceiling cleaned in the years 1967 to 1969, and gave the library its new name "The Asam Hall." This is one of the finest intact Baroque libraries in Germany, having retained its original 12,000 books, its frescoes, decoration, and shelves. Many of the books are priceless.

(Above) At the height of his family's power, Prince Carl Anselm von Thurn und Taxis (1733–1805) was Postmaster General of the German Reich as well as of Burgundy and the Netherlands, and between the years 1773 and 1797 he served as High Commissioner of the Imperial Diet.

(Opposite) The entrance to the south wing is embellished with a sumptuous staircase that rises three stories, at the foot of which stands a statue of Hermes. The staircase is sheathed with multicolored marble and its wrought-iron banister, forged by the Regensburg master David Nordemann, is punctuated by lapis lazuli columns. Another entrance corridor (below), in Renaissance style, displays flags with the family coat of arms. Both entrances lead to plush apartments (overleaf) that display the art collections of the Thurn und Taxis family. On the left, a chinoiserie panel, circa 1738, from a Porcelain Cabinet previously in the Frankfurt palace, stands next to a portrait of Princess Helene von Thurn und Taxis, sister of the Habsburg Empress Elizabeth of Austria. On the right are Portuguese blue-and-white tiles, or *azulejos*, possibly brought to Regensburg by one of the Infantas of Portugal who married into the family.

of visitors in the large courtyard where they enjoy such fare as Shakespeare's *Romeo and Juliet*, Hofmannstahl's *Jedermann*, or Mozart's *The Magic Flute* in a special adaptation for children, or big time rock bands. Between performances, they lunch at a brauhaus, which was made out of one of the family's breweries just outside the castle walls, go sightseeing, have picnics, and visit the Thurn und Taxis museums which include one for the family's coaches and sleighs and another that displays its collection of eighteenth-century snuffboxes, jewels, silver, and gold plate. Among the snuffboxes is one of heliotrope and gold, studded with large diamonds, created for Frederick the Great in 1770, and others that various Russian emperors gave to Thurn und Taxis princes during state visits. As Johannes once explained, "Frederick the Great had a superb collection, as did Catherine the Great, and Napoleon. When my grandfather went to visit the Tsar in St. Petersburg, he would give the emperor jeweled crosses or medallions and elaborate snuffboxes, and the tsar gave him even lovelier snuffboxes and Fabergé objects in return. It was a nice way to say you enjoyed the stay and that he hoped to see you again. That's the way our collection of boxes began." And then there are the diamond and precious stone encrusted medals, such as the Order of the Golden Fleece, that were first given the family in 1642, ecclesiastical jewelry, and a black caftan embellished with diamond buttons that is every bit as grand as that of King Augustus the Strong, which is on display in Dresden's Green Vault (page 168). The late prince Johannes was as enthusiastic and knowledgeable about gems as an Oriental satrap, and once said, "As a connoisseur of beautiful things, I especially love my jewels. And above all I love the pieces that belonged to my ancestor Queen Marie-Antoinette of France.... If I look at a great sapphire or ruby, I don't rush to the laboratory to see if the light refracts in a special way. I rely on a feeling that comes from my ancestors and on my own microscopic vision."

Who were these ancestors who made the modern prince and his heirs so rich and self-indulgent? The first we hear of the Taxis family is in northern Italy in the twelfth and thirteenth centuries where they went by the name of Tasso. The paterfamilias seems to have been Rainerio di Tasso, who was a judge in the suite of Queen Mathilde, the consort of Emperor Heinrich IV. At the time, the family lived in Cornello, a small mountain village in the Valley of Brembana near Bergamo. Dominating their little village and its fortifications was Monte Tasso, the Badger Mountain, from which they took their name. The inhabitants of the little village in this sparse mountain landscape produced sturdy couriers who were hired as messengers by the Republic of Venice, the Papal States, and the Duchy of Milan. The late Prince Johannes put it somewhat differently, "Instead of stealing, the sons and grandsons of Rainerio charged what today would be called protection money, making sure that carriages and their contents arrived safely." As of 1490, some family members set up as messengers

in Innsbruck, Malines (Mechelen), and Brussels, then under Burgundian and Spanish control, while others were employed in Frankfurt and Regensburg. King Maximilian, Regent of the Tyrol, asked the Tasso family (known as Taxis in the north) to create a posting system whereby relays were set up at thirty-seven kilometer intervals, where horses and riders changed and the mail rushed around Europe. This was rather like the Pony Express in the Wild West and the beginning of the enormous and highly profitable middle European mail system of the Taxis family—who were soon to be given the privilege of adding "von" to their name, the first step in a rapid ascent to becoming Princes of the Holy Roman Empire.

In the seventeenth century, the family came up with a perhaps tenuous link to the Milanese Torriani family, also known as della Torre, who had ruled over Milan and Lombardy until they were expelled by their ducal rivals, the Viscontis. The Thurn und Taxis convinced the Emperor Ferdinand II to legitimize the newly discovered link, and so the Tassi or Taxis could now be called Torre e Tasso in Italy or Thurn und Taxis in northern Europe, and their new coat of arms included a torre (tower) and a tasso (badger). Rubens designed the cartoons for a set of tapestries that would to hang in their new Brussels palace, including the scene of the marriage of Leonhard II and Alexandrine, battles between the Viscontis and the della Torres, and the new coat of arms. Some of these are still hanging at the family schloss in Regensburg. The family had got to the top in a bit over a century, moved their headquarters to Frankfurt in 1702 and in 1731 started work on a magnificent palace on the elegant Eschenheimergasse that was designed by Robert de Cotte, the architect of France's King Louis XV.

The opening of the palace coincided with the Pragmatic Sanction of 1740. The Habsburgs occupied Bavaria, the homeland of the Wittelsbach Holy Roman Emperor Charles VII who thus moved his court to Frankfurt, and in 1745 Prince Alexander von Thurn und Taxis (1652–1714), the Wittelsbach's Postmaster General, was made Permanent Resident to the Emperor's Diet that had been meeting at Regensburg since 1663. His job involved reflecting the glory of the monarch to the Diet's members, a position that the prince could carry out magnificently, thanks to his immense fortune, by organizing balls, shooting parties, sleigh rides in the snow, and musical and literary evenings. The Comédie Française gave performances at Regensburg as did several Italian opera companies, and during the lifetimes of Prince Alexander Ferdinand and his son Karl Anselm von Thurn und Taxis (1733–1805), Regensburg became the political and social center of the Holy Roman Empire.

The French Revolution caused an immense upheaval, and Napoleon was soon off to conquer all of Europe. The Holy Roman Empire fell in 1806, and the Thurn and Taxis lost their postal empire in Bavaria and Napoleon adopted a policy of

(Above) A detail of the stove in a salon on the first floor of the south wing, circa 1890, in the international neo-Baroque style prevalent during this period. Of the same period and style is the south wing's dining room (opposite), prepared for a small lunch party.
The south wing's reception rooms are incredibly opulent; practically all the walls are upholstered in red silk and covered with family portraits. The butler is dressed in the traditional family blue livery used since the eighteenth century.
(Left) The eighteenth-century court dress of Prince Carl Anselm von Thurn und Taxis, highlighted by the emerald and diamond Order of the Golden Fleece, diamond buttons, and swaggers. This, along with the family snuffboxes, gold and silver plate, and other treasures, is now in the St. Emmeram Museum.

The late Prince Johannes and his wife Princess Gloria (left) await their guests in the Palm Room (overleaf, left), which is filled with nineteenth-century antiques and family photographs. The palm tree was inspired by George IV's Brighton Pavilion. (Opposite) The bedroom of Johannes's grandmother Princess Margerete, an Austrian Grand Duchess whose mother was the sister of the late Austrian Empress Elizabeth; Margerete married Prince Albert von Thurn und Taxis in 1890 and she bore a striking resemblance to her great, great aunt Queen Marie-Antoinette of France. (Overleaf, right) The sinuous Golden Staircase that leads up to the elaborate and highly gilded stucco Porcelain Cabinet on the floor above, where a great amount of Chinese and Japanese ceramics are hung on the walls and spread about on neo-Baroque tables and consoles. Nineteenth-century German neo-Louis XV furniture prevails in the Smoking Room (above).

secularizing religious institutions, which was carried out by Count Mongelas. So, in 1812, as compensation for the postal monopoly, the Thurn and Taxis were given the medieval St. Emmeram monastery which they then rebuilt as the present five-hundred room hodgepodge of medieval, Gothic, Sun King, Louis XV, Empire, and Napoleon III styles that became the main Thurn und Taxis residence. The Wittelsbach Court decorator Leo Klenze worked on the medieval cloister, interspersing Revivalist Gothic corridors, chapels, and statuary among fine period carvings, and creating a dramatically lit sepulcher for the Thurn und Taxis family tombs—which, at the time, might have seemed odd as they were just unpacking in the newly redesigned castle. The east wing became the ceremonial center of the house, with an *enfilade* of reception rooms up to that of any European court. The Frankfurt palace was stripped of much of its paneling, which was cut down to fit the lower ceilings at St. Emmeram, and soon there was a white and gold mirrored rococo ballroom, a throne room, a silver gilt rococo salon inspired by the Blue Cabinet in Nymphenburg's Amalienburg, a family chapel, and lots more.

The last of the postal empire was sold to Prussia for three million thalers on July 1, 1867, and shortly afterwards Prince Maximilian Maria (1862–1885) started building the south

(Above) The bust of Princess Margerete is to be found in the middle of her studio in the south wing of the house. She and her husband were the first of the family to make good use of the newly designed, opulent, Gilded Age rooms of the south wing. They established the highest standards of entertaining among Europe's royal and aristocractic families, which they kept up even as the world changed around them. They had six sons, two of whom—Prince Franz Joseph and Prince Karl August—headed the princely family, but neither left a male heir in his wake, thus breaking the family line for the first time. Princess Margerete was known as a devoted mother, a very accomplished artist, a social worker, and a skilled equestrian. She painted and sculpted and had several exhibitions of her fine watercolors. The Prince was eulogized as, "an aristocrat with true nobility of heart, a true representative of Western civilization and thought, a patron of the arts and sciences, a supporter of the poor and needy." Their balls and shooting weekends were among the summits of pre-war social life, and guests invariably gathered at the elaborate bowling alley (opposite) in the south wing, where the names of winners of tournaments were inscribed on panels in gold letters; hunting trophies line the walls. There is also an indoor swimming pool. (Overleaf) The family living room is known as the Salon Rothschild, since Princess Gloria's main advisor on the interior decoration after she got married was the Paris tastemaker Baroness Liliane de Rothschild. They went together through the seemingly endless works of art and furniture in the house to choose what would make up a cosy, cohesive ensemble. As Princess Gloria said at the time, "I've been digging around in the cellars and found thousands of objects that my husband's grandfather considered merely tons of junk."

wing with his architect Max Schultz. The now fully ensconced family really needed a comfortable place to live and entertain in the comfortable Gilded Age style of Victoria and Albert or Napoleon III and his Empress Eugénie, a style that was taken on by the Rothschilds and American robber barons. This meant marble-faced entrance halls and corridors, walls covered in red silk, tufted sofas and chairs, lots of paintings in heavy, gilded frames, family portraits galore, oriental carpets, newly-commissioned crystal chandeliers and, for the country, stuffed birds and rows of stag horns that boasted of the family's penchant for mass extermination of any game in the forest. These great entertaining spaces were now where everybody gathered for the *diners de chasse* in white tie and tails, floor length gowns, jewels, and tiaras.

Prince Max built an elaborate bowling alley where many a duchess could be seen after dinner using her left hand to hold up her skirt and hang on to her tiara and her right hand to roll those heavy balls down the alley. These rooms were finished in 1891, giving their builder no time to enjoy them. That was the pleasure of Prince Albert I (1867–1952), who lived on quite happily through the upheaval of Europe's monarchies, and through two hideous world wars, hardly changing his royal lifestyle. Albert was married to a Habsburg archduchess, Margarete, a skilled artist whose atelier has been kept in the house as a memorial to her (page 174). He was so distinguished and aristocratic that no trappings of royalty were needed to underline his deeply blue blood. His oldest son, Prince Franz Joseph inherited the title at the age of 59. Franz Joseph and his brother Karl August both married daughters of the King of Portugal. Franz Joseph's son and only heir Gabriel was killed at the Battle of Stalingrad in 1942, and so the title and the fortune passed to Karl August and through him to Prince Johannes, with the family proviso that he marry and have a male heir.

Johannes was a playboy of the Western world and marriage was not high on his list of priorities. He was having too much fun for that, but a fortune estimated at three billion dollars was hanging in the balance. So, he married Princess Gloria and never spent a dull moment. They went on a three-month Mediterranean cruise in Johannes's 130-foot yacht *Aiglon*, and then they flew to Brazil to look at a few hundred-thousand-acre estates that had been inherited from the royal Portuguese relations. Back in Regensburg, Princess Gloria, young and full of fun, rode around the countryside incognito with her brother asking the local farmers in her drawling Bavarian brogue what they thought of the new princess. And when Johannes was sixty in 1988, she gave him a legendary party at Schloss Emmeram. The courtyard was turned into a medieval market place with hundreds of the locals in traditional Bavarian costume, there was a performance of *Don Giovanni* with the Munich Opera, and Gloria changed the plot, stopping the furious Commendatore from taking Don Giovanni down to

hell by shouting out, "No, you can't kill him. I will save him." At which point the band in the ballroom broke out into the old Marlene Dietrich song, "Johnny, wann du Geburgstag hast" sung by Gloria. The audience was dressed in eighteenth-century costumes and included Mick Jagger and Jerry Hall, Malcolm Forbes, Alfred and Judy Taubman, and many other distinguished guests. Gloria was soon nicknamed "Princess TNT" by the press, and she and Johannes became the hottest society couple of the day. Their lives would be followed closely in *W*, *Point du Vue*, *Olá*, *Vanity Fair*, *Vogue*, and a host of other magazines and journals. Invariably, Johannes had a large red carnation in the boutonnière of his Caraceni suits or dinner jacket and Gloria was bedecked in the family jewels and always seemed to be having a good time.

She gave Johannes children, including the son who legitimized his rights to the title and fortune. And as a well-born, even if slightly outrageous, central European aristocrat, Gloria knew the importance of "kinder, küche, und kirche" (children, kitchen, and church), and she gave direction and a center to her rather demanding and spoiled husband's life. They grew ever closer through the short time they were married, and when Johannes was close to death, they both realized what a deep and satisfactory union they had enjoyed.

The immensely rich Johannes thought he was a great businessman and failed to follow his father's sound advice to go hunting or shooting but not to become a banker. Influenced by the lives of the powerful friends he met in New York, he decided to modernize the family finances, hired professional managers, and then borrowed money on his vast forests to buy American businesses and real estate. Soon a leading German business publication documented mismanagement and severe disagreements between the family and the trust that held everything for the benefit of the heirs. As one of the richest families in Germany, the TNTs were suddenly off the society pages and making headlines in *Forbes* and the *Wall Street Journal*. When Johannes died in 1990, the German government hit the estate with an enormous bill for inheritance taxes. And thus the government took the snuffboxes, silver, and gold as partial payment, and created a museum on the property. Princess Gloria, who had never been considered a businesswoman, was suddenly thrust into the position of protecting her children's inheritance. She took crash accounting and finance courses, asked her friend Alfred Taubman, the shopping mall king and owner of Sotheby's, to look into her situation and give her his best advice, and with time, courage, and patience she worked it all out. But first went the family jewels, auctioned off at Sotheby's in one of the most heralded sales of our time. Ever the good sport, Gloria said, "Let's face it, we don't wear tiaras so often, so why keep so many." On the block was a sumptuous diamond and pearl tiara made by the court jeweler Lemmonier for the Empress Eugénie and worn by Gloria at her wedding; it was acquired by the Louvre. Also on

A decorative, wrought iron, art deco style staircase (above and opposite) goes up to what are today the private family apartments as well as a series of guest bedrooms. Until the arrival of Princess Gloria, this area of the house consisted of a rather uninteresting series of 19th century bedrooms located over the old cloister. These were completely gutted and rebuilt into far more contemporary quarters, mostly by the African born Irish decorator Gabhan O'Keefe. Princess Gloria has used the staircase and the private rooms to display her own collection of contemporary art, a project which was warmly supported by her husband. She called it "The Gloria School of New Expressionists".

She bought works by Donald Baechler, Takashi Murakami, and Paul McCarthy among others, and also became interested in such video artists as Bill Viola. Photographic portraits of the princess and her children hang on the walls of the staircase. (Below) another view of the more traditional Rothschild salon.

Gabhan O'Keefe , the London based decoprator, was described by Bob Colacello in *Vanity Fair* as "possibly the most original, and certainly the most talked about decorator of the 90s." The rooms he decorated for Princess Gloria were her private suite which consists of a bedroom (above and opposite, and a bathroom (left) flanked by deep reveals and door cases, whose centerpiece is a black basalt bathtub. There is also a boudoir and a dressing room. Nearby, O Keefe also designed for her a particularly sumptuous Chinese Room and Library. The curtains of the library were made up of especially designed Lampas silk from Lyon, and drip with faceted crystal drops of colored glass as well as crystal beads painted in gold. As O'Keefe likes to say, "The trick is to know prercisely where the line is drawn between grandeur and vulgarity."

offer were the twenty-seven-karat emeralds of the Russian Grand Duchess Vladimir, a nine-row diamond "dog collar" with matching bracelets, and another three hundred lots estimated in the tens of millions of dollars.

The next year at St. Emmeram, there was a house sale of carloads of family furniture from different family palaces, which was gobbled up at wild prices by celebrity-struck and aristocracy-yearning yuppies. This time, Gloria said, "I want to do nothing except what is necessary right now, and that is to take care of the kids and the business. I slept at school, I married a rich man, and now I have to work. It's all right". More than all right. Following the lead of Princess Alexandrine Thurn und Taxis who pulled the family chestnuts out of the fire in the seventeenth century, the present Princess also saved the family fortune, and she has brought up her well-balanced children in an atmosphere that could mildly be described as eccentric, and she will soon see black ink on the last line of the accounts of the vast white elephant of a family house that she so enjoys.

PALÁCIO FRONTEIRA

The Perfect Portugese Manor House

The façade of the Fronteira palace (above) seen from the Great Garden (preceding pages). On the first floor are the windows of the house's library, and below them the terrace of an apartment occupied by the cousin of the Marquis de Fronteira, the palace's present owner. The adjacent façade has been made into an exceptionally beautiful walkway designed in the seventeenth century by Alexis de Jantillet. Effigies of Roman gods in niches (opposite) stand on bases and a waterspout in the center of a seashell below them shoots up water. On each side of the gods are azuleijos of female representations of the liberal arts and above them are terracotta effigies of Roman emperors set into della Robbia-like wreaths. Some of the statues are reflected in the glass panels of French doors leading into the reception rooms of the house (left). One door leads into the delightful Sala de Batalhas (overleaf, right), named after the skirting of azuleijo scenes of the principal events of the Portuguese Wars of Restoration with Spain. Also seen here is the humorous equestrian portrait in stucco of Dom João de Mascarenhas, second Count of Torre and builder of the Fronteira palace.

In the late nineteenth century, a traveler named Ramallho Ortigão wrote in his *Guide to Portugal*, "Although so fallen from its former importance in the fickle and capricious opinions of the capital's high society, the old and friendly town of Benfica is still a little suburban retreat from Lisbon. It carries the same prestige that Tivoli and Frascati must hold for Rome. In no other place in Portugal, with the exception of Sintra, can there be found in so small an area such beautiful, historical, anecdotal and nostalgic quintas as in Benfica. . . . They approach, nearly joining in a sweet murmur of water, splashing in the springs or running and bubbling into the dripping garden earth. Orchards and vegetable gardens, in a perennial greenness of rural and luxurious vegetation, give forth a bucolic perfume, as do the flowers and fruits."

Today, Benfica is part of a far larger Lisbon, and the Palácio Fronteira of the present Marquis of Fronteira and Alorna is a few minutes drive from the very center of town along one of the many super highways that link Portugal together. There is still a small orchard behind the house, but instead of the bucolic setting that was here a hundred years ago, the magnificent formal gardens now look out on high-rises. But such is the beauty of the Palácio Fronteira that one practically never looks beyond its walls. The house is endowed with one of the finest collections of *azuleijos*—Portuguese ceramic tiles—in the world, remarkable frescoes, among the best stucco decoration in Portugal, as well as eighteenth-century statuary in the garden and on the terraces. One of the most beautiful *quintas* in the country, the house is open to the public a few hours a day, but has few visitors and has maintained the atmosphere of a private house.

Rooms that are visited run into those that are not, and one wing of the house is lived in by Dom Fernando José Mascarenhas, twelfth Marquis of Fronteira, thirteenth Count of Torres, fourteenth Count of Asumar, Lord of the Palácio de Saõ Domingos de Benefica, and much more. His large living room, known as the Sala de Aparato, was largely decorated by Pedro Alexandrino with mythological scenes framed with elaborate lemon-and-white rococo stucco inset with fresco medallions of Roman portraits. This decorative program covers the walls and the ceiling, and seeming to support it are scenes in eighteenth-century azuleijos of the hunt and other diversions of the countryside. Off the main living room of Dom Fernando's apartment is a small dining room with his collection of fine Portuguese silver, which is also used as a conference room to discuss the affairs of the foundation that manages the palace. The marquis' salon is filled with eighteenth-century furniture, Old Master paintings, and Compagnie des Indes

(Above and preceding pages left) After entering the courtyard of the north façade of the palace, inspired by the Italian architect Sebastiano Serlio and large enough to hold twenty carriages, visitors make their way to an unusual staircase leading to the first floor reception rooms. A marble fountain with dolphins and a representation of Neptune is inset into a niche lined with blue-and-white *azuleijo* tiles (preceding pages, left) in a camellia pattern that covers the walls of the staircase as well. A broad white marble balustrade makes its way up the stairs and lines the upstairs landing, which is decorated with stucco moldings and faux marble panels. One end of the landing leads into a sun-filled, arched library whose walls are completely lined with bookshelves. The celestial globe is by William Cary (1759–1825), family photographs are set out on the lid of an old piano, while Oriental carpets and other Mascarenhas family antiques fill out this attractive room.

porcelain, which was always a favorite of Portuguese collectors. The same can be said of two fine adjacent rooms, the frescoed Sala de Juno or Imperial Salon and its antechamber, the Salon of the Four Elements, which is skirted with blue-and-white tiles and a portrait of the renowned general, the third marquis of Alorna. The public can visit these rooms during the day and often Dom Fernando entertains his guests here in the evening. This part of the house was built in 1770 by the fifth marquis, in order to accommodate his large family and household all year long rather than just from May to October, which was the case before the great earthquake of 1755 practically destroyed Lisbon. Like a similar disaster in San Francisco, the conflagration caused by candles and lamps did as much damage as the quake itself. The Mascarenhas town palace went up in flames as did the family archives, and the marquis moved to his country estate. In this old part of the house, there is an apartment that is occupied by cousin José Maria Mascarenhas and his wife, Doña Maria Assunção, which has a bright sunlit living room with a skirting of *azuleijos* painted in a panoply of colors (unlike most others in the house, which are blue and white), vitrines displaying a collection of decorative fans, cozy Napoleon III armchairs, and comfortable, large upholstered sofas. Adjacent to the living room is an elegant library and a

formal barrel-vaulted dining room. All around are fine examples of Portuguese ceramics and family photographs, and French doors open onto an expansive terrace with steps leading into the magnificent Jardim Grande.

Dom José Maria runs the large family farm in the Alentejo, about 100 miles from Lisbon. The Mascarenhas once had many such farms, but some were confiscated and made into public land in the 1940s while others were taken away during the Communist revolution that started on April 25, 1974. Dom Fernando received a degree in philosophy from the University of Lisbon, where he studied from 1963 to 1969, while participating in leftist movements both in Portugal and as a student in Paris—in what the French call "the events of 68." He became a member of the Portuguese Democratic Movement in 1969 and then joined the Democratic Movement of Opposition, and after the revolution he became Interim General Secretary of the Social Democratic Movement. The marquis also organized secret meetings in the house. One meeting was broken into by the police and caused a scandal in Lisbon society. Dom Fernando now likes to speak of himself as the equivalent of a Russian Octobrist revolutionary. Like them, he was a member of one of the country's most noble and established families, and therefore sat on both sides of the fence. Notwithstanding all this subversive activity, in 1970 Dom Fernando decided to take charge of the Benfica property instead of going to Oxford or Cambridge to pursue a life of the mind.

In 1974, workers occupied the land but the marquis continued to live in the house, which they left alone. When there was a break in the revolution in 1975 and elections in 1976 that voted out the Communists, he had to fully assume the burden of his inheritance. "It is my life's work," says Dom Fernando. "If you have taken the decision yourself, it is as much a pleasure as a burden. I felt the need to be part of something greater than myself, and I found this in the context of the house. You have no choice, and you do what is necessary." His fondness for the Palácio Fronteira was not really a new discovery. When he was eight, Dom Fernando's father referred to it as "my house," and the son furiously replied, "No, it's my house!" He was put in the corner until he got out of the jam by admitting it was "their house." Without the surrounding income-producing land and with all the expenses a large quinta entails, Dom Fernando considered selling the Palácio Fronteira, but asked a larger price than anybody would pay. The Brazilians considered making it their embassy, and the Portuguese Republic considered it as a replacement for their palace at Belém. However, the marquis finally put the property into a foundation and sold so much of its furniture and treasures that he was surprised it all had fit into Fronteira in the first place. He used the money to transform part of the palace into rental apartments, let out the quarters currently occupied by his cousin, and somehow

(Opposite) The Sala dos Paneis, which became the house's main dining room. When the palace was built, meals were served all over the house on tables put up for the occasion, and this was one of many all purpose salons. The tiles of mythological, rural, and hunting scenes skirting the room are Dutch rather than Portuguese, quite a rarity, and they may be the first such tiles imported into Portugal. Several Alorna family portraits hang on the rococo stuccoed walls, and the centerpiece of the dining room table is an Empire *surtout de table* by one of France's finest silversmiths, Philippe-Pierre Thomire (1751–1843). (Above) A dining room cabinet is filled with Portuguese plates with floral motifs. (Left) A rococo table stands against the *azuleijo* tiles in the dining room.

The dining room leads to a series of salons in the new wing of the house that are essentially the private apartments of Dom Fernando, the tenth Marquis of Fronteira and Alorna, and these include the Sala de Apparato, his main living room (opposite), a small dining room (page 196), the Sala Impero (pages 198, 199), the Sala de Fumo, the Sala de Eros, and a delightful rustic corridor (page 200), off which is a large kitchen with a full-time chef.

The Sala de Apparato (opposite) is in the marquis' wing, which he shared with his mother until her death. It was built after the great earthquake and fire of 1755 that destroyed a large part of Lisbon and forced many aristocratic families to seek refuge in their country estates. The Fronteira palace was too small to accommodate such a large household all year around and had to be expanded. The stucco decoration and frescoes are of extremely high quality, and the marquis has made himself very much at home, adding his books, collections of minerals (above), family photographs (right), a large television set, and comfortable sofas. He is seated in the foreground playing solitaire; cards are one of his favorite pastimes. A man of immense erudition, Dom Fernando's writings and opinions are very much respected among Portuguese intellectuals.

life went on. When things picked up, the foundation rented the palace out for parties and meetings, and today there is a waiting list to get in. Doña Maria helps make the menus, which are catered by a company she organized and runs, orders the flowers, arranges the waiters, picks the finest Mateus wines, and does whatever else is necessary for a glamorous evening. The foundation also has afternoon recitals of mostly classical music followed by dinner and poetry readings, which are particularly appropriate as one of Dom Fernando's ancestors, the Marchioness of Alorna, was a very well-known Portuguese poetess who introduced German Romanticism into Portugal. The foundation has done well enough to keep up the large gardens, restore the house, and even buy fine antiques to replace those that were sold.

Manor houses, such as the Palácio Fronteira, were once the center of the country's rural life, but are no longer the setting for the social life of a landed aristocracy as they once were. The institution of the manor house developed in the Middle Ages, when Portugal was a perpetual battleground between Moors and Christians as well as between Spain and Castille. They featured defensive towers, often made of wood and other perishable materials that gradually disappeared or were integrated into the plan of larger houses. These show the influence of ancient Rome in layout and purpose, the Italian Renaissance in architectural vocabulary, eighteenth-century France in formal parterres, the rococo in the use of shells, and Islam in the importance of water in the gardens. They are called villas, solars, quintas, montes, or palácios, depending on their location and grandeur. In Brazil, where the Portuguese manor house was introduced by colonial grandees, they are known as *fazendas*. These manor houses reflect the Greco-Roman tradition of building villas and gardens as places for meditation and enjoyment; remains of such villas from Roman times were found in the Portuguese ruins of Conimbrigia and suggest a high degree of sophistication.

A contemplative walk, or *ambulatio*, through the house and garden is at the very heart of enjoying a humanist villa, so let us enter the Fronteira palace through the main gate, crowned by sculptures of Mars and Venus, and continue into a symmetrical and harmonious courtyard, where twenty carriages could once be accommodated for distinguished visitors. The north façade seen here is a sober design of Palladian arches and square windows, inspired by the work of Sebastiano Serlio (1475–1554), well known for his book *The Five Books of Architecture*, published in England in 1611. The wing erected after the earthquake of 1755 is on our right, and on our left is a plain wall with a small door that leads into the Jardim Grande—a classical garden framed by terraces, its walls embellished by blue-and-white *azuleijos*—which features a remarkably elaborate, two-story pavilion framing a large body of water. Stone benches are placed along the walls, and most of this lower garden is devoted to a large, formal, brilliantly designed, geometric parterre of trimmed

Dom Fernando's dining room contains part of his collection of Portuguese and French silver. The Portuguese royal family and aristocracy were among the most important collectors of silver in Europe, and Lisbon's museums are filled with masterpieces of silversmiths such as Thomas Germain and Pierre-Philippe Thomire. When the Armenian billionaire Calouste Gulbenkian came to reside in Lisbon, he brought with him a great quantity of Romanoff silver that he had purchased from the Soviet government—and Lisbon became the most important center for these courtly delights.

and tamed boxwood hedges punctuated by lead statuary, topiary bushes, and clusters of red roses. Visitors are propelled along gravel paths through this elegant composition at the center of which is placed a tall fountain. These parterres rival those of great French châteaux or renowned Florentine and Roman villas, although the garden itself also shows Arab influence. Islamic gardens were generally self-contained, walled in, a world unto themselves. They have nothing at all in common with English gardens by the likes of Capability Brown, who brought the house into the countryside with large, open vistas featuring naturalistic clumps of trees, lakes, bridges, follies, temples, or even mausoleums. Water, a central element of the Arab house, was particularly cherished for its scarcity in dry climates, and gardeners knew very well how to channel and preserve this precious commodity. Storage tanks were essential, as can be seen in the gardens of the Alhambra in Granada, the Generalife in Seville, the Alcázar of Córdoba, or elsewhere. In the case of the Palácio Fronteira, a fantastic pavilion was erected to embellish the large holding tank, or pool—which has been made into a decorative body of water open to the sky that is like a great mirror reflecting the light.

At the edge of this rectangular pond is a balustrade that winds around the grand staircases of the pavilion's identical twin

The Sala de Juno or Empire Salon is quite formal thanks to its Napoleonic decoration, and it is filled with Louis XVI furniture and Compagnie des Indes porcelain. This was made in China in the Portuguese taste, and highly appreciated by Portugal's aristocracy and high bourgeoisie. Over the fireplace is a large painting by Pelligrini of three family siblings: Dom José Trazimundo, seventh Marquis of Fronteira, Doña Leonor Mascarenhas, who was to become the wife of the Count of Alva, and Dom Carlos Mascarenhas. The present marquis entertains his friends here at night, but the room can be visited by tourists during the day.

towers that flank each side of the upper terrace, and that continues along the walkway of the King's Gallery of the pavilion. The lower parterre is decorated with Velázquez-like equestrian images of members of the Mascarenhas family in large blue-and-white tiles, framed in arches covered with shell-encrusted decorative stone, which Portuguese artisans borrowed and transformed from the grottoes of Italian country villas, which had become very popular in the sixteenth century. This decoration, much used at the Fronteira palace, reflects the Portuguese taste for Oriental artifacts and the country's links with India. It enhances the magical atmosphere that pervades the Fronteira palace by breaking up surfaces into shimmering light.

The gallery of marble busts of Portugal's kings on the upper terrace of the pavilion starts with Dom Enrique and ends with Dom Pedro II as Prince Consort. These statues are set into framed niches lined with a highly reflective pine-cone motif in glazed copper ceramic, rather like lusterware and perhaps of Spanish origin. After walking along the terrace, we come upon a high tiled wall, dappled with sunlight, which passes through tall and leafy trees. Here are more royal effigies, in this case those of Dom João V, Dom José, Doña Maria I, and Don João VI. Below is the Garden of Venus, and further along the Casa de Água, also known as the Casa do Fresco, a wonderful, grotto-like sanctuary totally covered by rocaille decoration that includes porcelain plates and precious ceramics smashed into smithereens. In front of this folly is a very unusual fountain with marble tritons, curlicues, and tiled benches. Above is a terrace with the family swimming pool and the Lago dos Pretos, a later water tank embellished with mythological figures. These overgrown and casually kept gardens are filled with lush semitropical plants, and the mix of exotic vegetation with the Italian Renaissance canon is very unusual and seductive, as if Florence's Boboli Gardens had been moved to Bahia in Brazil. This secluded part of the house, on a higher level than the far larger gardens below, was where the ladies could come without special permission from their husbands, a sort of seraglio that reflects the segregation of men and women in this Islamic-influenced part of the world. The lower garden is

The living room of the marquis' cousin, Dom José, and his wife, Doña Maria Assunção, in the main house, facing the Great Garden. Dom José is responsible for running the family properties and Doña Maria takes care of renting out reception rooms of the palace for gala occasions. She has started her own company for catering these events. The apartment is comfortably furnished, has unusual colored *azuleijos*, a collection of Compagnie des Indes porcelain, and antique fans.
(Opposite) A long corridor in the new wing, lined with *azuleijos*, is in character with more modest Portuguese quintas and is, in fact, adjacent to the kitchen.

a more public place, formal and European, while the upper garden is private, exotic, tropical, and mysterious.

A few steps away is a vaulted staircase that leads to a small chapel with an inscription dating it to 1584, which would indicate that it was built nearly a century before the palace itself. It contains a few oil paintings, tile panels, and two altars built in 1771, the year the fifth Marquis of Fronteira married, and is dedicated to Saint Francis Xavier and Saint Anthony. Just outside the chapel is a long, broad walk way designed by Alexis de Jantillet which might be considered the most original, enchanting, and decorative feature of the entire complex. The wall of the house is a long gallery with nine life-size marble effigies of Saturn, Mars, Jupiter, and other gods in niches, each with a large seashell basin at the foot, which conceals a powerful waterspout. These niches are set into a series of large blue-and-white *azuleijo* arches, representing female personifications of the liberal arts: astronomy, geometry, rhetoric, music, and others. In the interstices between the arches are relief portraits of Roman emperors set into della Robbia-like round wreaths of lush and colorful fruit. Another touch of color is added by geraniums growing in *azuleijo* planters at the feet of the Liberal Arts. "On the opposite side," writes de Jantillet, "along the whole of the length of the walk, there is a gallery of very beautiful marble containing vases with flowers and benches ready to receive those people who are tired out from walking." The vegetation is tropical and lush, the statues are reflected in the glass of large French doors, the light changes throughout the entire day, and the entire terrace can best be described as sumptuous. The garden walk ends here, and the French doors lead us back into the old wing of the house. The first salon one encounters is perhaps the most striking. This Room of Battles features *azuleijos* depicting the main episodes of the Wars of Restoration between Spain and Portugal. Above them is wonderful, vibrant stuccowork including a large, delightful equestrian portrait of Dom João de Mascarenhas, second Count of Torre and builder of the Fronteira palace. This portrait is placed directly over a representation of the battle of Ameixial, in which he participated. Stucco decoration, including portraits of other family members, richly covers the entire vaulted ceiling of this gala room, which is unfurnished except for a few tapestries, since it is used for conferences and large dinners. The room, in turn, leads into a sort of grand entrance hall at the top of the main marble staircase, from which one enters the library on the right and the Sala dos Panéis, used as a dining room, on the left. The library is filled with sun thanks to floor-to-ceiling windows that look onto the Great Garden. Its shelves contain about five thousand books (many dating to the sixteenth century), family archives, as well as correspondence. There are fine antiques, and family photographs, many more than one hundred years old, are set out on the top of a nineteenth century piano. The dining room is distinguished by its Dutch tile wain-

The water tank of the Jardim Grande (above and overleaf) is the main feature of the Fronteira gardens. It is, in effect, a small man made lake that reflects the sky as well as a series of equestrian portraits of the Mascarenhas family in blue-and-white *azuleijos* that are part of a pavilion with a pair of balustraded staircases leading to the Gallery of Kings on the first floor. The balustrade knits together this highly imaginative creation. The gallery (left) contains a series of twenty four marble busts of Portugal's kings (opposite), starting with Count Dom Pedro Henriques, father of Dom Alfonso Henriques, and ending with Dom Pedro II as Prince Regent. The gallery continues into the upper garden where there are further statues inset into an *azuleijos* wall.

scoting, the only non-Portuguous tiles in the house. In fact, these may well be the first Dutch panels marketed in Portugal, and they consist of mythological events, country life, and hunting scenes. The pastel stucco from the eighteenth century, and the dining table has a sumptuous *surtout de table* by Pierre-Philippe Thomire, the finest silversmith of the French Empire period.

What is life like today in this grandest of Portuguese country houses? A fully staffed office in a wing downstairs deals with the affairs of the family foundation, making money from renting the rooms, and spending it on cultural programs, restoration, and maintenance. Dom Fernando plays bridge on many afternoons in his sumptuous salon, visits his properties, entertains his friends, reads and writes a great deal. He is soft-spoken, witty, charming, professorial, and highly respected in Portugal's intellectual world for his vast knowledge in many areas. Doña Maria makes sure that everything is ready for the people or companies that will be renting the house for an evening. The foundation is very conscious of its cultural role, and carefully screens those who want to rent the house. On elegant or prestigious evenings, the Fronteira palace rediscovers its original purpose of giving pleasure to its owners and their guests. If the group is small, they might dine in the Sala dos Panéis by candlelight, while the Room of Battles will take up to sixty for dinner. For more than a hundred, additional tables can be set up outside on the adjacent walkway in the company of the Roman generals and the Liberal Arts ladies, each table displaying a beautiful, flowered centerpiece. Recently, a Portuguese art dealer who lives in London put up a single long table for 150 of his friends along the Gallery of Kings in the Great Garden in the manner of eighteenth-century banquets at Versailles. Guests in evening dress made their way up the opulent marble staircase set into *azuleijo*-covered walls after wandering through the salons and gardens with a glass of champagne in hand. The full moon rose, everybody made their way up the two formal staircases to their places, and the Fronteira palace again worked its spell. Despite earthquakes, wars, and revolutions, the house is still very much alive and can be as seductive as it was in its heyday.

In the upper garden, a private and secluded place in which women were free to mix with men despite the Islamic constriction to do so, there is the very unusual Casa de Água or Casa do Fresco (opposite), decorated inside with a fantastic variation on the man-made grottoes in Rome, or Giuliano Romano's grotto at Palazzo Te in Mantua. It is, in fact, a chapel. The Portuguese artisans added bits of broken Oriental porcelain (some reputed to have come from plates used at Portuguese inaugural banquets), broken black glass, and chips of flint in addition to the usual shells and fragments thereof. This flashy and shimmering decoration certainly reflects the Portuguese interest in the art of India, where they ruled over Goa. In front of the Casa is a very unusual basin (above).

Acknowledgments

Owning or, even worse, having to keep up a great ancestral home has always been a difficult proposition. Enemies once attacked with armies and cannon fire, revolutionaries stormed the gates, governments confiscated land or attempted to collect taxes and inheritance duties. Families fought for control while nature waged an unending battle and acres of roof constantly needed repairing. Many gardeners, cooks, maids, and footmen are needed to maintain the style of life for which stately homes were built, and one wonders why the descendents of the original owners do not simply give up and stop sacrificing their fortunes and peace of mind to continue a lifestyle that has been of the past for nearly a century.

The answer is undoubtedly ancestor worship. Palace building is the most fundamental expression of power. It can be seen clearly in the vast houses being built today in Palm Beach, Dubai, or in the suburbs of Moscow. It was once evident on New York's Fifth Avenue, which, in the 1890s, resembled a condensed tour through the Châteaux of the Loire. But the houses of the newly rich have never been able to boast of a gloriously long dynastic history, and that is what the owners of the splendid palaces seen in the preceding pages do not want to give up. They will marry dollar or peso heiresses, dispose of the family jewels, auction off their furniture, sell entrance tickets, open zoos and cafeterias, put on pop concerts, petition ministers, beg the local government for support, rent out their rooms of state for company meetings, let in the local butcher for his daughter's wedding. They have created trusts, foundations, and have adopted high profiles in order to increase the flow of visitors to their now often public properties—and keep living in them. Many of these visitors are on the lookout for a live prince or duchess walking their dog, like tourists on safari in the Serengeti who drive around the arid plains looking for the few remaining leopards. And the visitors imagine that somewhere, in an area of the house they will never be invited to, life goes on as it once did. In some houses, it does indeed, although the footmen are now hired by the day rather than for life, and often the hosts are entertaining tycoons who have rented the stately pile for a shooting weekend.

This book is about eight great family houses and their owners, all of whom have preserved their heritage. They are friends, and they have allowed me along with photographer Marc Walter to roam around their houses. They have decorated beautiful dinner and tea tables with the family porcelain and silver, arranged flowers, brought out family photographs, and often as not invited us to stay. They have allowed me to interview them and they have been invariably helpful and supportive, as have their staffs. Their support system, depending on how the house functions today, can range from a mere handful to over a hundred, and in attempting to thank everybody I will invariably forget some. So, allow me to try to do so in the order of their appearance in the preceding pages, and also to mention the main sources that I consulted.

The Kasteel de Haar, near Utrecht, is one of Holland's most popular castles. It is closed all of August so that its owner, Baron Thierry van Zuylen, may have four house parties of around twenty people each, and he kindly invited Marc and me to come while he was entertaining. I am indebted to Baroness Gabrielle van Zuylen who lent me the oversize, two-volume limited edition *Kasteel de Haar* by J. Cuypers, the architect of the castle, a publication commissioned by Baron Thierry's grandfather, Etienne. My thanks also go to Mr. Hinse for sending us the excellent booklet on the castle and other materials published for visitors.

The Casa de Pilatos, in the heart of Seville, is an amazing amalgam of Gothic, Moorish, and Mudéjar styles, and it is the property of the Fundación Casa Ducal de Medinaceli, presided over by the eighteenth duchess, Victoria Eugenia, and directed by her third son, Ignacio, the Duke of Segorbe. The duchess still lives in a wing of the house, which she allowed us to photograph. Don Ignacio spent endless hours with me, clarifying the history and genealogy of one of Spain's oldest and most noble families, and his wife Gola filled the house with beautiful roses from her country house near Córdoba, took out beautiful "mantones," wedding dresses, and fans from her mother-in-law's closets to lend local color to our photographs, and set tables in the traditional Sevillana manner for tea parties and Jerez with tapas. The best books on the house, both of which I mined, are *La Casa de Pilatos* by Vincente Lleo Canal and a shorter book with the same title assembled by the family foundation. My great appreciation goes to Susanna, who arranged every detail of our visit, corrected my manuscript, and recommended publications for my research. Don Ignacio housed us in his wonderful hotel La Juderia very close to his own palace, which is made up of an assemblage of medieval houses, and is one of the most delightful *hôtels de charme* in all of Europe.

The Earl and Countess of Harewood still occupy an entire floor of their large Palladian house in Yorkshire, and have worked hard to preserve its private character in their public rooms. I would like to thank them for joining this effort, for being so supportive, and to thank Lord Harewood for his corrections to and appreciation of my text. Particular thanks go to Terence Suthers, John Martin, and their wonderful staff who facilitated our work. The many booklets published for visitors to Harewood were full of useful and informative information on the house as was *Harewood House* by Mary Mauchline, *The English Country House: A Grand Tour* by Gervase Jackson-Stops and James Pipkin, *Great Houses of England and Wales* by Hugh Montgomery-Massingberd, and *The Englishman's Room* edited by Alvilde Lees-Milne.

At the Château de Haroué, the chatelaine, Princess Minnie de Beauveau Craon, put us up in her wonderfully livable château and set beautiful tables for our dinners and lunches. Her cook Eveline and her butler Julien were unfailingly attentive, and her friend Bruno Roy arrived with a car full of fresh flowers from Paris, which he arranged beautifully throughout the house. We thank them all for their hospitality, enthusiasm, and effort. The best book on the castle, *Haroué. Demeure des Princes de Beauveau Craon*, was produced at Minnie's initiative and was our main source of information.

The renowned Palazzo Gangi, where Luchino Visconti filmed the great ball scene of his cinematic version of Giuseppe Lampedusa's *The Leopard*, now belongs to Giuseppe Vanni Calvello, Prince of Gangi, and his beautiful French-born wife Carin. The house is their passion, and Carin recreated the atmosphere of the grand days of the house for us by opening up drawers that hid menus and seating plans of dinner parties of the past, by arranging flowers in the sumptuous Sicilian manner throughout the house, and by setting out baroque Sicilian pastries on the family porcelain—all this while receiving and guiding two large groups of visitors whose contributions help maintain this stately palace. Angheli Zalapi has written an excellent book called *Palaces of Sicily*; it includes an introduction by Gioacchino Lanza Tomasi, a learned musicologist and historian who is related to practically every grandee on the island. Gioacchino is the director of the Teatro San Carlo in Naples and took time from his busy schedule to write our piece on the Palazzo Gangi, for which I am deeply appreciative.

The Palazzo Sacchetti on the Via Giulia in Rome is steeped in the history of the city and of the Vatican, and I am indebted to the Marchese and Marchesa Sacchetti for giving us the run of their magnificent palace, and will long remember the delicious lunch party that Giovanna Sacchetti arranged for me in the Great Gallery of the house while Marc was chasing the sunlight throughout the other rooms. An excellent scholarly book *Palazzo Sacchetti*, written by various authors, was published by De Luca Editori d'Arte in Rome and it was my main source of information, and De Luca very kindly lent us a few illustrations that are reproduced on pages 136, 137, 147, and 155.

St. Emmeram, in the ancient city of Regensburg in Bavaria, has been a home to the princely Thurn und Taxis family since they received it in the early nineteenth century as compensation for confiscation of the German branch of their postal empire. Princess Gloria von Thurn und Taxis, the present chatelaine, agreed immediately to our inclusion of her house in this book, allowed me to interview her at great length, placed at our disposal her extremely affable and knowledgeable assistant Count Soden, and decorated two festive tables—one for Christmas dinner, the other for a shooting party—which are included here. The best books on the house are *Das Fürstliche Haus Thurn und Taxis* by Martin Dallmeier and Martha Schad, *Thurn und Taxis Museum* by various scholars with an introduction by Reinhold Baumstark, and the official guide to the palace. I took much from these sources, and appropriated witty quotes from interviews of the late Prince Johannes by Prince Michael of Greece, Peter Dragadze, and Bob Colacello.

The last house to appear in the book is the Palácio Fronteira in Benfica, once a bucolic retreat and today a suburb of Lisbon. The present marquis, Dom Fernando José Mascarenhas lives alone in one wing and his cousin José Maria and his wife Doña Maria Assunção live in another part of the house. They have all been extremely hospitable and helpful, and Dom Fernando's tales of his days as a leftist revolutionary are fascinating. The monograph on the house entitled *The Palace and Gardens of Fronteira* by José Cassiano Neves was very useful to me, as was *Portuguese Gardens* by Helder Carita and Homen Cardoso.

Particular thanks go to Marc Walter, the photographer and art director of this book; to Thomas Neurath at Thames & Hudson who is co-publishing it; to Marike Gauthier at Le Passage in Paris who is publishing the French edition; to Mark Magowan, my partner at the Vendome Press, for supporting this project; and to Christopher Sweet who edited the text.

First published in the United States of America
by in 2006 by
The Vendome Press
1334 York Avenue, New York, NY 10021

Copyright © 2006 The Vendome Press
Text copyright © 2006 Alexis Gregory
Photographs copyright © 2006 Marc Walter

Library of Congress Cataloging-in-Publication Data

Gregory, Alexis.
Private splendor : great families at home /
by Alexis Gregory and Marc Walter.
p. cm.

ISBN-13: 978-0-86565-170-8 (hardcover : alk. paper)
ISBN-10: 0-86565-170-1 (hardcover : alk. paper)

1. Palaces--Europe. 2. Nobility--Europe--Anecdotes. I.
Walter, Marc. II.
Title.
NA7710.G74 2006
728.8094--dc22
2006018620

10 9 8 7 6 5 4 3 2 1

Designed by Marc Walter / Chine, Paris

Printed in Spain